# TEACHING STUDENTS
## WITH
# LEARNING DISABILITIES

# A Practical Approach to Special Education for Every Teacher

*The Fundamentals of Special Education*
A Practical Guide for Every Teacher

*The Legal Foundations of Special Education*
A Practical Guide for Every Teacher

*Effective Assessment for Students With Special Needs*
A Practical Guide for Every Teacher

*Effective Instruction for Students With Special Needs*
A Practical Guide for Every Teacher

*Working With Families and Community Agencies to
    Support Students With Special Needs*
A Practical Guide for Every Teacher

*Public Policy, School Reform, and Special Education*
A Practical Guide for Every Teacher

*Teaching Students With Sensory Disabilities*
A Practical Guide for Every Teacher

*Teaching Students With Medical, Physical, and Multiple Disabilities*
A Practical Guide for Every Teacher

*Teaching Students With Learning Disabilities*
A Practical Guide for Every Teacher

*Teaching Students With Communication Disorders*
A Practical Guide for Every Teacher

*Teaching Students With Emotional Disturbance*
A Practical Guide for Every Teacher

*Teaching Students With Mental Retardation*
A Practical Guide for Every Teacher

*Teaching Students With Gifts and Talents*
A Practical Guide for Every Teacher

# TEACHING STUDENTS WITH LEARNING DISABILITIES

A Practical Guide for Every Teacher

JIM YSSELDYKE
BOB ALGOZZINE

**CORWIN PRESS**
A SAGE Publications Company
Thousand Oaks, California

*For information:*

Corwin Press
A Sage Publications Company
2455 Teller Road
Thousand Oaks, California 91320
www.corwinpress.com

Sage Publications Ltd.
1 Oliver's Yard
55 City Road
London EC1Y 1SP
United Kingdom

Sage Publications India Pvt. Ltd.
B-42, Panchsheel Enclave
Post Box 4109
New Delhi 110 017 India

Printed in the United States of America

**Library of Congress Cataloging-in-Publication Data**

Ysseldyke, James E.
Teaching students with learning disabilities: a practical guide for every teacher / James E. Ysseldyke & Bob Algozzine.
  p. cm.
Includes bibliographical references and index.
ISBN 1-4129-3949-6 (cloth) — ISBN 1-4129-3902-X (pbk.)
  1. Learning disabled children—Education. I. Algozzine, Robert. II. Title.
LC4704.Y78 2006
371.9—dc22

2005037825

This book is printed on acid-free paper.

06  07  08  09  10  9  8  7  6  5  4  3  2  1

| | |
|---|---|
| *Acquisitions Editor:* | Kylee M. Liegl |
| *Editorial Assistant:* | Nadia Kashper |
| *Production Editor:* | Denise Santoyo |
| *Copy Editor:* | Marilyn Power Scott |
| *Typesetter:* | C&M Digitals (P) Ltd. |
| *Indexer:* | Kathy Paparchontis |
| *Cover Designer:* | Michael Dubowe |

# Contents

About *A Practical Approach to Special
Education for Every Teacher*     vii
  Acknowledgments     viii

**About the Authors**     xi

**Self-Assessment 1**     1

**Introduction to *Teaching Students
With Learning Disabilities***     5

1. **What Are Learning Disabilities?**     7
  Criticism of the Definition     8
  Criteria for Identification     8

2. **How Common Are Learning Disabilities?**     11
  Rapid Growth in the Category     11
  Explanations of the Category's Growth     12

3. **What Causes Learning Disabilities?**     15

4. **How Are Learning Disabilities Assessed?**     17
  What Is Unique About Learning
    Disability Assessments?     18
  Trends in the Assessment Process     19

5. **What Characteristics Are Associated
   With Learning Disabilities?**     21
  Cognitive     22
  Academic     23
  Physical     23
  Behavioral     23
  Communication     24

6. **How Do Teachers Teach Students With Learning Disabilities?** 25
   Improving Basic Skills 27
      *Reading* 27
      *Math* 32
      *Written Language* 33
   Improving Classroom Behavior 35
      *Work Habits* 35
      *Study Skills* 37
   Improving Social Relations 39

7. **What Should Every Teacher Know About Learning Disabilities and ADHD?** 43
   Definitions of ADHD 43
   Principles of Remediation 46
      *Inattention* 46
      *Excessive Activity* 47
      *Impulsivity* 47

8. **What Trends and Issues Influence How We Teach Students With Learning Disabilities?** 49
   A Changing Definition 50
   Subtypes of Learning Disabilities 51
   Definitions Vary by State 51
   Transition Questions 52

9. **Learning Disabilities in Perspective** 53

10. **What Have We Learned?** 55
   Key Points 55
   Key Vocabulary 56

**Self-Assessment 2** 59

**Answer Key for Self-Assessments** 63

**On Your Own** 65

**Resources** 67
   Books 67
   Journals and Articles 67
   Organizations 68

**References** 71

**Index** 73

# About
# *A Practical Approach to Special Education for Every Teacher*

*Special education* means specially designed instruction for students with unique learning needs. Students receive special education for many reasons. Students with disabilities such as mental retardation, hearing impairments (including deafness), speech or language impairments, visual impairments (including blindness), emotional disturbance, orthopedic impairments, autism, traumatic brain injury, other health impairments, or specific learning disabilities are entitled to special education services. Students who are gifted and talented also receive special education. Special education services are delivered in many settings, including regular classes, resource rooms, and separate classes. The 13 books of this collection will help you teach students with disabilities and those with gifts and talents. Each book focuses on a specific area of special education and can be used individually or in conjunction with all or some of the other books. Six of the books provide the background and content knowledge you need in order to work effectively with all students with unique learning needs:

Book 1:   The Fundamentals of Special Education

Book 2:   The Legal Foundations of Special Education

Book 3:   Effective Assessment for Students With Special Needs

Book 4:   Effective Instruction for Students With Special Needs

Book 5:   Working With Families and Community Agencies to Support Students With Special Needs

Book 6:   Public Policy, School Reform, and Special Education

Seven of the books focus on teaching specific groups of students who receive special education:

Book 7:   Teaching Students With Sensory Disabilities

Book 8:   Teaching Students With Medical, Physical, and Multiple Disabilities

Book 9:   Teaching Students With Learning Disabilities

Book 10:  Teaching Students With Communication Disorders

Book 11:  Teaching Students With Emotional Disturbance

Book 12:  Teaching Students With Mental Retardation

Book 13:  Teaching Students With Gifts and Talents

All of the books in *A Practical Approach to Special Education for Every Teacher* will help you to make a difference in the lives of all students, especially those with unique learning needs.

# ACKNOWLEDGMENTS

The approach we take in *A Practical Approach to Special Education for Every Teacher* is an effort to change how professionals learn about special education. The 13 separate books are a result of prodding from our students and from professionals in the field to provide a set of materials that "cut to the chase" in teaching them about students with disabilities and about building the capacity of systems to meet those students' needs. Teachers told us that in their classes they always confront students with special learning needs and students their school district has assigned a label to (e.g., students with learning disabilities). Our students and the professionals we worked with wanted a very practical set of texts that gave them the necessary **information about** the students (e.g., federal definitions, student characteristics) and specific **information on** *what to do about* **the students** (assessment and teaching strategies, approaches that work). They also wanted the opportunity to purchase parts of textbooks, rather than entire texts, to learn what they needed.

The production of this collection would not have been possible without the support and assistance of many colleagues. Professionals associated with Corwin Press—Faye Zucker, Kylee Liegl, Robb Clouse—helped us work through the idea of introducing special education differently, and their support in helping us do it is deeply appreciated.

Faye Ysseldyke and Kate Algozzine, our children, and our grandchildren also deserve recognition. They have made the problems associated with the project very easy to diminish, deal with, or dismiss. Every day in every way, they enrich our lives and make us better. We are grateful for them.

# About the Authors

**Jim Ysseldyke, PhD,** is Birkmaier Professor in the Department of Educational Psychology, director of the School Psychology Program, and director of the Center for Reading Research at the University of Minnesota. Widely requested as a staff developer and conference speaker, he brings more than 30 years of research and teaching experience to educational professionals around the globe.

As the former director of the federally funded National Center on Educational Outcomes, Ysseldyke conducted research and provided technical support that helped to boost the academic performance of students with disabilities and improve school assessment techniques nationally. Today he continues to work to improve the education of students with disabilities.

The author of more than 300 publications on special education and school psychology, Ysseldyke is best known for his textbooks on assessment, effective instruction, issues in special education, and other cutting-edge areas of education and school psychology. With *A Practical Approach to Special Education for Every Teacher,* he seeks to equip educators with practical knowledge and methods that will help them to better engage students in exploring—and meeting—all their potentials.

**Bob Algozzine, PhD,** is Professor in the Department of Educational Leadership at the University of North Carolina at Charlotte and project codirector of the U.S. Department of Education–supported Behavior and Reading Improvement Center. With 25 years of research experience and extensive first-hand knowledge of teaching students classified as seriously emotionally disturbed (and other equally useless terms), Algozzine is a uniquely qualified staff developer, conference speaker, and teacher of behavior management and effective teaching courses.

As an active partner and collaborator with professionals in the Charlotte-Mecklenburg schools in North Carolina and as an editor of several journals focused on special education, Algozzine keeps his finger on the pulse of current special education practice. He has written more than 250 manuscripts on special education topics, authoring many popular books and textbooks on how to manage emotional and social behavior problems. Through *A Practical Approach to Special Education for Every Teacher*, Algozzine hopes to continue to help improve the lives of students with special needs—and the professionals who teach them.

# Self-Assessment 1

Before you begin this book, check your knowledge of the content being covered. Choose the best answer for each of the following questions.

1. Which one of the following methods would NOT be a means of identifying students with learning disabilities?

   a. Showing that a child demonstrates a developmental delay

   b. Providing evidence that a child has a process disorder

   c. Providing evidence that a child has not responded to generally effective instruction

   d. Demonstrating that a child presents a discrepancy between academic achievement and intellectual ability

2. The definition of children with learning disabilities includes those _____ .

   a. with mental retardation

   b. who have writing difficulties

   c. with severe visual impairment

   d. who come from disadvantaged families

3. From 1990 to 2003, what was the increase in the number of school-aged children identified with learning disabilities?

   a. 30%

   b. 40%

   c. 50%

   d. 60%

4. What is the problem with assessing for processing disorders as a basis for identifying children with learning disorders?

    a. It is time consuming.

    b. Children may be negatively affected by such tests.

    c. The measurements of such disorders are inadequate.

    d. The cost is beyond the means of the average-income family.

5. Using curriculum-based measures, teachers are able to identify children whose _____ and rate of performance are below those of their classmates.

    a. Level

    b. Height

    c. Quality

    d. Frequency

6. What kind of information is gathered from a functional behavioral assessment?

    a. The specific skills that a student is able to perform

    b. The factors that cause the occurrence of a behavior

    c. The effectiveness of a behavior intervention program

    d. The level at which a child is functioning in the classroom

7. In _____ programs, students are taught reading skills by actually using them, together with other communication skills.

    a. Analytical

    b. Comprehensive

    c. Structured

    d. Whole-language

8. One way to avoid the use of liberal eligibility criteria in the identification of learning disabilities is to ensure that a characteristic used in the criteria is both _____ and specific.

   a. Holistic

   b. Objective

   c. Observable

   d. Universal

9. _____ activities, such as getting children to talk about their hobbies, encourage students with disabilities to be integrated in a class.

   a. Alternative communication

   b. Cooperative

   c. Inclusive

   d. Socializing

10. Which one of the following traits is NOT considered a primary feature in the criteria for identifying children with ADHD?

   a. Adaptability

   b. Hyperactivity

   b. Impulsivity

   c. Inattention

# REFLECTION

After you answer the multiple-choice questions, think about how you would answer the following questions:

- Define specific learning disabilities as stated in the 1997 reauthorization of IDEA. Give three problems associated with the definition.
- There has been a rapid growth in the number of students identified with specific learning disabilities. What do you think are some reasons for this phenomenon?
- Briefly describe one strategy you would use to help a child

  a. With reading difficulties

  b. Who lacks study skills

  c. Who has difficulty paying attention in class

# Introduction to Teaching Students With Learning Disabilities

**Mark** is a fifth grader with a learning disability. His school performance illustrates a pattern common to many students with learning disabilities: persistent difficulty learning to read. Now Mark can read third-grade material reasonably well, but he still has problems comprehending what he has read. His spelling is a little better than his reading, but his handwriting is still very messy and immature. Mark spends most of his time in a general education classroom with his neighborhood peers. His teacher describes him as "likable and very interested in learning." She says that Mark's classmates sometimes complain about his frequent asking of questions and that they "now and then" avoid him during independent activities, free time, and recess. She is working with Mark to help him improve his peer relations. Mark is earning passing grades in math, science, and social studies with assistance provided by general and special education teachers (e.g., taped texts, modified tests, and a homework buddy).

*P*uzzling is a term teachers sometimes use to describe Mark. Some people say students like Mark have hidden disabilities because their strengths in some areas often mask or hide learning problems in others. Perhaps you know a person who is quite bright but who has trouble mastering skills that come easily to others. Students who have these difficulties are sometimes identified as having learning disabilities. They may not learn in the same ways or as easily as their peers. They may have special needs that sometimes pose problems in large classes in which most students perform reasonably well with minor assistance. Often teachers are challenged to modify instruction so that students who learn differently from the majority of the class still receive the assistance they need. The Bringing Learning to Life box below describes how Mark's teachers made an accommodation that helped him succeed.

## Bringing Learning to Life: Helping Mark to Read Using Taped Texts

Mark's teachers have found that tape-recording passages from textbooks is an effective way to help him compensate for his learning disability. They conducted an informal assessment to determine if Mark learned best with or without the text in front of him as he listened to the tape. He did better just listening.

Mark's teachers chose the material to be recorded and then prepared the tapes. In some cases, they recorded only key sections of the text; in others, they recorded entire chapters and passages. Sometimes they added tips to the tapes to encourage Mark to review the material after critical sections or to remind him to take notes on important parts of the lessons. One time, they added comprehension questions to provide practice recalling facts during the lesson. Mark reported that this was very helpful. Whenever possible, the teachers had classmates do the taping during independent work times.

# 1

# *What Are Learning Disabilities?*

A lthough no definition of *learning disability* is universally accepted, every state in the United States delivers services to students who have learning disabilities or one of its substitute terms, such as *perceptual and communication disorders*. In general, students identified with specific learning disabilities are those who are performing poorly in some academic area. They present a discrepancy between actual performance and the level at which professionals and parents think they should achieve, and this discrepancy is not due to any identifiable disability.

Most states use the definition specified in the guidelines and regulations that accompanied the Individuals With Disabilities Education Act (IDEA) or a definition that will produce an equivalent population. At the time we write this book, IDEA has been reauthorized. We expect it will take a year or two to produce the regulations and guidelines that actually have the most impact on practice. So until new regulations and guidelines are written, educational professionals are relying on the federal guidelines for the 1997 reauthorization. According to those guidelines, a *specific learning disability* means

> a disorder in one or more of the basic psychological processes involved in understanding or in using language, spoken or written, which may manifest itself in imperfect ability to listen, think, speak, read, write, spell,

or to do mathematical calculations. The term includes such conditions as perceptual handicaps, brain injury, minimal brain dysfunction, dyslexia, and developmental aphasia. Such a term does not include children who have learning problems which are primarily the result of visual, hearing, or motor handicaps, of mental retardation, of emotional disturbance, or of environmental, cultural, or economic disadvantage. (U.S. Department of Education, 1997)

# CRITICISM OF THE DEFINITION

When this definition was first proposed, many educators deemed it vague and unacceptable. Three problems were most troublesome. First, the definition caused a rift between those who supported the importance of identifying underlying causes of learning disabilities, such as psychological processing disorders, and those who did not. Second, the definition alienated adults with learning disabilities by referring only to children. Third, the definition included an ambiguous exclusion clause that did not clearly state that learning disabilities can exist with other disabilities but cannot be the result of them. This created confusion in the field.

# CRITERIA FOR IDENTIFICATION

To address some of these concerns, the U.S. Department of Education has specified criteria to be used in identifying students with learning disabilities. A team of professionals who have a variety of experiences with the student as well as assessment information must determine if the student does not achieve at a level judged appropriate. The team looks at one or more of the following areas:

1. Listening comprehension

2. Oral expression

3. Written expression

4. Basic reading skill

5. Reading comprehension

6. Mathematics calculation

7. Mathematics reasoning

In making the decision, the team is permitted to search for a discrepancy between academic achievement and intellectual ability in at least one of the seven areas. A student is not identified as having a specific learning disability if the discrepancy between ability and achievement is primarily the result of another disability, such as a visual, hearing, or motor disability, mental retardation, or emotional disturbance, or if it is due to perceived environmental, cultural, or economic disadvantage. With the new reauthorization of IDEA, Congress eliminated the demonstration of a discrepancy as a criterion and gave school districts permission to identify students as learning disabled (LD) when they failed to respond to evidence-based instruction (instruction that previously has been shown by researchers to work with other students their age).

The discrepancy criterion was removed as a requirement because professionals cannot agree on the magnitude of the difference between expected and actual achievement necessary for a student to be identified with specific learning disabilities. Some states had been using one grade level and others used at least two; some states used 15 standard score points and others used 23 or 30. When the specific criteria vary, different numbers and types of students are provided special education services. Specific criteria for identification as LD under the new legal requirements have not yet been specified; there is no official definition of failure to respond to appropriate instruction and for that matter, no definition of appropriate instruction. So the jury is still out on whether the new rules will resolve the difficulties apparent in implementation of discrepancy formulas.

# 2

# *How Common Are Learning Disabilities?*

S tudents with learning disabilities are the largest group receiving special education services in the United States. About 4 percent of the school-aged population received special education services under the category of specific learning disabilities (U.S. Department of Education, 2002). This is a large group: about 1 or 2 in every class of 25 to 35 students. Of the 5.8 million students ages 6 to 21 who received special education, about 50 percent (2.9 million students) were included in the specific learning disabilities category.

About 45 percent of students with learning disabilities are served in general education settings. They spend less than 21 percent of the school day outside their general education classroom or resource rooms. Only 15 percent of students with learning disabilities spend more than 60 percent of the school day outside their general education classroom (U.S. Department of Education, 2001).

## RAPID GROWTH IN THE CATEGORY

Since the passage of the Education for All Handicapped Children Act (1975), the number of students served in special education in the category of specific learning disabilities has more than doubled. This dramatic increase has not occurred in any other category. The number of students in this category has increased while the number of students in other categories has decreased. From 1977 to 2003, the number of students with learning disabilities more than doubled (100 percent increase) and the number of students with mental retardation was cut in half (50 percent decrease). From 1990 to 2003, there was more than a 30 percent increase in the number of school-aged children identified with learning disabilities.

The percentage of students with disabilities (ages 6 to 21) who were identified with specific learning disabilities during the 2000–2001 school year is presented in *Table 2.1*. Column 4 shows that, in each state, approximately half of all students with disabilities are included in the category of specific learning disabilities. The distribution across states ranged from about 25 percent in Kentucky to over 60 percent in Delaware, Massachusetts, Nevada, and New Mexico. This variation occurs because definitions and identification practices vary from state to state; however, the steadily increasing numbers for learning disabilities is true in most states.

# EXPLANATIONS OF THE CATEGORY'S GROWTH

There are several explanations for the rapid growth in the numbers of students with learning disabilities; this growth has caused concern. In 1983 the National Association of State Directors of Special Education (NASDSE) attributed the increase to five factors:

1. Improved procedures for identifying and assessing students

2. Liberal eligibility criteria

3. Social acceptance or preference for the learning disabled classification

4. Cutbacks in other programs and lack of general education alternatives for students who experience problems in the general classroom

5. Court orders making other classifications more difficult to justify

**Table 2.1**   Percentage Distribution of Students With Specific Learning Disabilities in the United States

| State | All Disabilities* | Specific Learning Disabilities** | Learning Disabilities as Percentage of All Disabilities |
|---|---|---|---|
| Alabama | 11.36 | 5.17 | 45.5 |
| Alaska | 11.55 | 6.62 | 57.3 |
| Arizona | 9.18 | 5.38 | 58.6 |
| Arkansas | 10.83 | 4.54 | 41.9 |
| California | 9.03 | 5.33 | 59.0 |
| Colorado | 9.06 | 4.40 | 48.6 |
| Connecticut | 11.08 | 5.11 | 46.1 |
| Delaware | 10.92 | 6.59 | 60.3 |
| District of Columbia | 12.47 | 6.40 | 51.3 |
| Florida | 12.83 | 6.26 | 48.8 |
| Georgia | 10.28 | 3.24 | 31.5 |
| Hawaii | 10.59 | 5.20 | 49.1 |
| Idaho | 9.76 | 5.58 | 57.1 |
| Illinois | 11.71 | 5.90 | 50.4 |
| Indiana | 12.63 | 5.23 | 41.4 |
| Iowa | 12.47 | 6.31 | 50.6 |
| Kansas | 10.62 | 4.68 | 44.0 |
| Kentucky | 11.10 | 2.87 | 25.9 |
| Louisiana | 9.89 | 3.99 | 40.3 |
| Maine | 14.00 | 5.75 | 41.0 |
| Maryland | 10.55 | 4.59 | 43.5 |
| Massachusetts | 13.68 | 8.52 | 62.3 |
| Michigan | 10.72 | 5.03 | 46.9 |
| Minnesota | 10.57 | 4.20 | 39.7 |
| Mississippi | 9.95 | 4.85 | 48.7 |
| Missouri | 12.16 | 6.27 | 51.6 |
| Montana | 10.18 | 5.58 | 54.8 |
| Nebraska | 11.97 | 4.93 | 41.1 |
| Nevada | 9.87 | 6.22 | 63.0 |
| New Hampshire | 12.07 | 5.83 | 48.3 |
| New Jersey | 13.86 | 7.50 | 54.1 |
| New Mexico | 12.80 | 7.69 | 60.0 |

*(Continued)*

**Table 2.1** (Continued)

| State | All Disabilities* | Specific Learning Disabilities** | Learning Disabilities as Percentage of All Disabilities |
|---|---|---|---|
| New York | 11.42 | 6.00 | 52.5 |
| North Carolina | 11.43 | 4.94 | 43.2 |
| North Dakota | 10.33 | 4.66 | 45.1 |
| Ohio | 10.42 | 4.07 | 39.0 |
| Oklahoma | 12.30 | 6.86 | 55.8 |
| Oregon | 11.30 | 5.71 | 50.5 |
| Pennsylvania | 10.15 | 5.66 | 55.8 |
| Puerto Rico | 7.42 | 4.11 | 55.4 |
| Rhode Island | 15.72 | 8.73 | 55.5 |
| South Carolina | 13.12 | 6.04 | 46.0 |
| South Dakota | 9.75 | 5.00 | 51.3 |
| Tennessee | 11.50 | 5.42 | 47.1 |
| Texas | 11.04 | 6.26 | 56.9 |
| Utah | 9.73 | 5.72 | 58.8 |
| Vermont | 11.73 | 4.49 | 38.3 |
| Virginia | 12.39 | 6.06 | 48.9 |
| Washington | 9.84 | 4.68 | 47.6 |
| West Virginia | 15.26 | 6.37 | 41.7 |
| Wisconsin | 10.96 | 5.20 | 47.4 |
| Wyoming | 11.87 | 5.94 | 50.0 |
| 50 States and D.C. | 11.05 | 5.52 | 50.0 |

*Percentage of school-age population (ages 6 to 21) receiving special education in all disability categories.

**Percentage of school-age population receiving special education in the category of specific learning disabilities.

*Source:* U.S. Department of Education (2002).

Fewer students are achieving at expected levels in general education. Identification of specific learning disabilities has become the preferred way to get help for them.

# 3

# *What Causes Learning Disabilities?*

Professionals have debated the causes of learning disabilities since the term was first used in the late 1960s. Today it is generally agreed that specific learning disabilities are the result of a neurological condition (National Joint Committee on Learning Disabilities [NJCLD], 2002). Yet there is little agreement on the methodology that school personnel should use to identify learning disabilities.

Although the NJCLD is composed of members of ten major organizations, it is safe to say that members of those organizations do not universally hold the neurological causation view. In fact, a significant number of school personnel believe that the majority of learning disabilities are the product of insufficient background experience, deficient learning experiences, or inappropriate instruction. Students who are learning disabled, then, are those who do not have other disabilities, are not considered disadvantaged, and for whom the educational system is not working effectively. Some of these students have neurological impairments.

Identification of learning disabilities should occur only after three steps have been taken:

1. Evidence-based practices have been implemented.

2. The student's progress has been monitored directly and frequently.

3. The student has been shown to fail to benefit from the instruction.

# 4

# *How Are Learning Disabilities Assessed?*

A ssessment practices used to identify learning disabilities now consist primarily of assessing and documenting students' response to intervention (RTI). School personnel provide students in general education settings with generally effective instruction. They monitor the progress of students in those settings in an effort to identify students who do not respond as expected. Those who do not respond get something else, or something more, from their teacher or from another educational professional. Again, progress is monitored, and those who still do not respond either qualify for special education or for special education evaluation (Fuchs, Mock, Morgan, & Young, 2003). As Speece, Case, and Molloy (2003) describe the process, teachers use curriculum-based measures in general education classrooms to identify children whose level and rate (slope) of performance are below those of their classmates. This dual discrepancy of level and slope becomes the marker by which to judge responsiveness to instruction. Dually discrepant children then receive general education instruction that is redesigned to meet their needs. This instruction and continued placement in general education would be treatment valid for children who demonstrate improvement and are no longer dually discrepant. For children who continue to demonstrate a dual discrepancy, the instruction and placement would not be valid, leading to a trial placement in special education to determine responsiveness and, hence, treatment validity, under more intensive instructional parameters (pp. 147–148).

A local education agency team, including teachers, parents, and other professionals, conducts a formal educational assessment to determine whether the student has a disability and to determine whether the student's individual needs justify special education services. A battery of tests may be used, or the team may use data derived by assessing responsiveness to instruction, and the team decides whether the student meets the state-specified criteria for being called learning disabled.

# WHAT IS UNIQUE ABOUT LEARNING DISABILITY ASSESSMENTS?

The assessment team must demonstrate that the student is performing poorly in school or at least not doing as well as professionals believe the student should do. Typically, this has been shown by measuring cognitive ability and academic achievement and determining that there is a significant discrepancy between the two. The magnitude of discrepancy necessary to be considered learning disabled differs from state to state. With the new IDEA reauthorization, school district personnel now may use the data derived from measuring RTI.

The team must also demonstrate that the disability is not due to a lack of instruction in reading or math or due to limited English proficiency. The disability must also be specific to certain educational content areas (e.g., reading) and not evidenced in all or nearly all areas. When students demonstrate deficits or difficulties across the board, then low achievement or mental retardation is the suspected condition.

The discrepancy between ability and achievement must also not be due to another disability (e.g., emotional disturbance or mental retardation) or to cultural deprivation or deficient experience. Many learning disability assessments include **measures**

**of process disorders**, such as auditory memory, grammatic closure, visual discrimination, or figure-background pathology.

## TRENDS IN THE ASSESSMENT PROCESS

In recent years, the process for declaring students eligible for learning disability services has changed. There has been a significant increase in direct and frequent measurement of academic progress (often called curriculum-based assessment) and the use of problem-solving methodology. Today it is common to employ diagnostic teaching, implement a variety of instructional approaches, and measure the extent to which the student profits from the instructional approaches before granting eligibility for special education services.

The use of **functional behavioral assessment** has also increased. In a functional behavioral assessment, assessors examine what happens before and after a student's specific behavior in order to identify factors that cause or support the occurrence of the behavior. Functional behavioral assessments are often carried out to rule out behavior disorders. **Functional academic assessments** are also often carried out to identify the extent to which evidence-based principles of effective instruction are being used to teach the student (Ysseldyke & Christenson, 2001).

# 5

## *What Characteristics Are Associated With Learning Disabilities?*

Learning disabilities may be identified at any age, but most are first noticed in the early elementary grades when teachers and parents become concerned about a child's school performance. For example, a bright, verbal child may be having difficulty learning the names of the letters of the alphabet, remembering the names of classmates, or learning to count to 20. Or a learning disability may be suspected if a child performs well in one area, such as reading, but poorly in others, such as math and handwriting. Or perhaps the child does well with written examinations but is not able to express ideas verbally. Often discrepancies are reflected in test scores (e.g., a fifth grader performs at the third-grade level in mathematics). In addition to test scores and general concerns about academic performance, a number of other characteristics of learning disabilities have been identified. These characteristics are grouped within the following five areas:

Cognitive

Academic

Physical

Behavioral

Communication

# COGNITIVE

Most professionals believe that students with learning disabilities have average or above average intelligence accompanied by specific cognitive, thinking, or psychological processing problems. These include problems remembering things, discriminating or differentiating between visual or auditory perceptions, and developing and using cognitive strategies. Students who have difficulty remembering what they see or hear will likely experience difficulty in school. Visual and auditory memory problems are associated with specific learning disabilities.

Perceptual problems are also associated with learning disabilities. These may occur in such areas as left-right orientation, figure-ground differentiation, pattern discrimination, body image, symbol recognition, and auditory association (associating sounds with symbols). Professionals have had considerable difficulty, though, developing adequate measures of these tasks and even more difficulty showing that improving perceptual problems produces related improvements in academic performance.

Students with learning disabilities are said to fail to develop and use cognitive learning strategies, such as organizing learning tasks and learning how to learn. There is evidence that successful learners employ a set of self-monitoring and self-regulating strategies that are absent or deficient in students with learning disabilities. Students with learning disabilities may lack awareness of the skills, strategies, and steps that are necessary to solve problems or complete tasks. They may also have difficulty evaluating the effectiveness of what they do.

# ACADEMIC

Students who don't perform as well in school as expected by their teachers or parents (based on their work with the student, the student's past performance, or an intelligence test score) may have a learning disability. Generally, discrepancies between expectations and performance are identified by comparing performance on standardized achievement tests with those of intelligence tests. Discrepancy between ability and achievement is a primary characteristic, but there is considerable debate about just how poorly a student must perform to be identified as having a specific learning disability. This debate translates into other interesting (mostly philosophical rather than practical) debates, such as, "Can students who are gifted and talented have specific learning disabilities?" and "Can students with mental retardation have learning disabilities?"

# PHYSICAL

Students with learning disabilities look like students who do not have them. Sometimes teachers of younger students report that they are more clumsy and awkward than their peers or that they demonstrate poor physical coordination and motor abilities. Sometimes they have good large-muscle coordination but difficulties in fine-motor coordination. Many of the tests used by schools to screen for learning disabilities include copying and tracing exercises to help teachers identify younger students who need remediation in these areas.

# BEHAVIORAL

Inability to attend to tasks (attention problems) and high rates of seemingly purposeless activity (hyperactivity-impulsivity) are behavioral characteristics commonly associated with learning disabilities. Students must attend to what is going on, listen to the teacher's lecture, keep their place in textbooks, and shift their attention among tasks when the classroom agenda changes. Students with learning disabilities may have difficulty coming to attention, focusing, and sustaining attention. Terms used to describe their behaviors include *inattention, hyperactivity, impulsivity, distractibility, daydreams, overly energetic,* and *erratic.* Terms might also include *disruptiveness* and *immaturity.* Professionals working with students who have behavioral challenges may not be sure whether the unwanted behaviors are causes of low academic achievement or the result of it. Many students with learning disabilities *do not* exhibit behavioral challenges, and many students that do not have learning disabilities *do* exhibit behavioral challenges.

Doing poorly in school is also related to problems with social behaviors and peer acceptance. Some of these characteristics include a lack of judgment in social situations (e.g., sharing personal information with strangers), difficulty deciding how others feel, interpersonal problems, problems establishing family relations, a lack of social competence in school, and low self-concepts.

## COMMUNICATION

At the preschool level, language problems are the most common characteristics found in students with learning disabilities. A disability may be suspected if a preschooler does not talk as well as expected, does not talk like his or her older brothers or sisters did at the same age, or does not respond adequately to statements and instructions.

Discrepancies between expected and actual language performance may also be evident in older students with learning disabilities who may have difficulty listening, speaking, defining words, and formulating linguistic constructions. Teachers, professionals concerned with speech and language problems, parents, and others who work with these students often focus their efforts on oral language difficulties. Sometimes they focus their work on written language difficulties as well.

# 6

## *How Do Teachers Teach Students With Learning Disabilities?*

The single, most fundamental characteristic of students with learning disabilities is a significant discrepancy between expected and actual performance in at least one academic content area. For this reason, academic instruction is the primary area in which students with learning disabilities require assistance.

Effective teachers provide direct instruction for skills students need to know, such as note taking and other study skills. They organize their instruction to help struggling students use their strengths and make up for their weaknesses. In addition, teachers of students with learning disabilities must modify their instruction to remediate problems and help the students compensate for skills they have not yet mastered. Administering unit tests in social studies orally is an example of how a teacher might help a student compensate for a learning disability in reading. *Table 6.1* lists general interventions used by teachers with students with learning disabilities.

Improving behavior and social relations is also part of effective teaching activities used with students with learning

**Table 6.1**　Ten Ways to Help Students Overcome Challenges Posed by Learning Disabilities

---

1. Provide alternative assignments to help students compensate for academic weaknesses.

2. Help students focus on relevant aspects of assignments.

3. Use concrete examples and demonstrations when teaching new content.

4. Provide opportunities for students to progress at their own rates.

5. Modify assignments to help students compensate for academic weaknesses.

6. Provide more opportunities for practice than required by peers.

7. Provide instructional aids (e.g., calculators, fact tables, spelling dictionaries) to help students compensate for academic problems.

8. Provide substitute materials in content area instruction with lower reading levels.

9. Modify tests and evaluation measures to compensate for learning problems.

10. Provide opportunities for self-monitoring.

---

disabilities. These students sometimes need help with classroom behaviors such as task avoidance, inattention, and hyperactivity. Many also have trouble organizing their time and using effective study skills; some have difficulty getting along with their peers. Teachers need to assist students in all areas of deficit. The guidelines that follow will help teachers work more effectively with students who have learning disabilities, by focusing on common areas of weakness:

Basic skills (reading, math, written language)

Classroom behaviors (work habits, study skills, social relations)

# Improving Basic Skills

Basic skills include the ability to listen, think, and speak as well as read, write, spell, and do mathematical calculations. Improving basic skills is a primary objective in teaching students with learning disabilities.

# Reading

Most elementary school programs rely on either analytical approaches or experience-based, whole language approaches when teaching students to read. In **analytical programs**, beginning readers are taught a systematic method for decoding words. Students are taught skills for attacking or breaking down words, then practice their decoding skills with words at appropriate instructional levels. Some analytic approaches rely on word families (*at: cat, fat, rat, hat, sat—The cat sat on the hat of the fat rat*) to teach the construction of meaning or comprehension from what is read.

In **whole language programs**, reading is integrated with other communication skills, especially writing. Students are taught reading skills by actually using them rather than by learning and practicing word identification skills. In whole language classrooms, teachers model reading and writing by reading aloud and telling stories to their students. Students choose some of their own reading and writing topics, and varied reading materials are present in their classroom libraries. Whole language instruction relies on reading and writing about actual personal experiences, rather than contrived stories or assignments, as its fundamental learning and meaning construction experience.

Educators have debated the value of word analysis versus experience-based instructional methods of reading instruction for decades:

The research . . . gives ample evidence that we do, indeed, know a great deal about beginning reading. Yet the divisiveness over code-emphasis [analytic approaches] versus meaning-emphasis [experience-based approaches] rages on. Isn't it time to stop bickering about which is more important? Isn't it time that we recognized that written text has both form and function? To read, children must learn to deal with both, and we must help them. (Stahl, Osborn, & Lehr, 1990, p. 123)

The following methods have been found to be effective in helping students with learning disabilities become better readers. They are grouped into three categories: sight word recognition, reading comprehension, and motivation.

## Sight Word Recognition

**1. Word Lists:** To improve sight word recognition, have students create their own reading practice sheets. Provide lists of simple words (e.g., need, cheer, light) and have students make new lists by adding word parts to each root word (e.g., needy, needed, unneeded, cheery, lightly). To make the activity more fun and integrate it with math, challenge students to find a specified number of words (e.g., 10, 20, 30), and have them keep track of their performance using weekly graphs. After the lists are completed, have students read theirs to a classmate. An alternative activity is to provide students with a word (e.g., harvest) and have them find other words by rearranging the letters (e.g., vest, rest, tar, hat, hear, hare, tare, tear, rate, rats, vase, aster, earth, stare, hearts, starve).

**2. Decoding Software:** Have students practice sight word recognition with computer programs. Use software like *Reader Rabbit* (The Learning Company) and *Word Munchers* (MECC) to help students learn decoding principles. They provide repeated practice formats that are highly motivating to many students.

## Reading Comprehension

**3. Repeated Readings:** To improve reading rate and comprehension, use repeated readings of the same passage. Select a passage of 50 to 150 words for each student that is at a level that is easily read. Have students read their passages orally three or four times. Keep track of the time required for each repeated reading. Also have students read their passages silently at least once a day. The goal for many students with learning disabilities is simply to practice reading more frequently. Repeated reading with high degrees of accuracy is an effective means of accomplishing this goal.

**4. Phonetic Cues:** Add cues to help students remember phonetic rules. Marking long vowels or combinations (read, reed), crossing out silent letters (take), and dividing words into smaller parts (com/pre/hen/sion) can be very helpful for students. Make up assignments with 15 to 20 practice words and have students read them at home for additional practice.

**5. Thematic Units:** Use thematic units to encourage social interaction and integration of reading with other areas of instruction. Reading activities, such as vocabulary study, study guides, spelling, comprehension activities, and reading guides, can be incorporated into a thematic unit on seasons, months of the year, holidays, outer space, farm animals, great literature, the continents, and other topics. For example, an integrated thematic unit on outer space might include writing stories; drawing constellations and labeling them; writing narratives of a space creature; listing facts about the earth and its features; experimenting with light, air, and water; creating illustrations of night and day in different parts of world; and creating a creature from another planet. The goal is to increase interest and comprehension of content as well as to provide practice reading.

**6. E-Books:** Use interactive computerized reading materials. An electronic book can contain the text of a story, pictures, sound effects, and movie clips of important scenes. The multimedia elements provide extra clues for comprehending the text and help to make the reading more interesting. Typically, students can click on unfamiliar words to get further visual or auditory information about it.

**7. Summaries:** Use writing to improve reading. After students have read a short passage, ask them to identify and make a list of relevant facts. Have them either write an outline of main ideas and supporting details or prepare an abstract using the facts, then write a summary. These assignments help students recall facts as well as improve their comprehension.

**8. Relevant Questions:** Use prompts to help students focus on relevant content. Select a reading passage that describes a central character engaged in an activity, and use the following questions as prompts for students to use while reading the passage:

- Who is the story about? Who is the central character?
- What does the central character do?
- What happens when the central character does it?
- What happens in the end?

**9. Minitests:** Make a reading assignment into a minitest that provides practice answering comprehension questions. Have students read a couple of the sentences and answer questions about them before reading the next section. See *Figure 6.1* for a sample minitest.

## Motivation and Interest

**1. Reading Aloud:** Reading to your students fosters an interest in reading. It shows students that reading is important and

**Figure 6.1**   Sample Minitests

**Comprehension Minitest 1**

*Read the following paragraph and answer the questions.*

Just about every Scout learned what to do for a snakebite: Cut open the wound and suck out the venom. Detailed instructions showing how to cut the bite marks with a sharp knife and how to pull the venom out were included in the Scout handbook.

1. What do Scouts learn to do for a snakebite?
2. Where were detailed instructions for this?

**Comprehension Minitest 2**

*Read the following paragraph and answer the questions.*

I never knew a Scout who was bitten by a snake, so I never knew if this would really work. I never tried it myself. I'm glad I didn't because now scientists say it is a bad idea to suck venom out of a snakebite.

1. When was the author bitten by a snake?
2. Should you suck the venom out of a snakebite?

has value. It also models reading with expression, fluency, interest, enjoyment, and variety. This helps students become more confident in selecting reading materials that meet their interests, skills, and needs.

**2. Learning Centers:** Classrooms that are literate environments teach students to value written words and encourage positive attitudes toward reading. Create a center that includes manipulatives for each content area (e.g., math, writing, reading, science, and social studies). Display books related to lesson themes, and supply plenty of writing materials to encourage students to write and draw at the center.

**3. Risk Taking:** Through the use of centers, many teachers encourage students with learning disabilities to feel comfortable making choices, taking risks, and experimenting with print media rather than constantly trying to avoid them. To encourage students to use print media and recognize their importance, label the items at each center.

**4. Nontraditional Materials:** Provide opportunities for students to read a variety of materials. When selecting materials, remember that reading something is better than reading nothing. Here are some examples of nontraditional reading materials that capture the interest of many students:

- Have students bring in booklets from their favorite CDs. Build reading activities around information on the covers and lyrics.
- Develop an interview sheet with questions about interests, hobbies, and special activities. Have students conduct interviews with each other. Create a scrapbook of completed interviews and make it available for students to read whenever they want.
- Survey students to determine their ten favorite TV programs. Ask a group of students to prepare a summary of the results using a line graph. Have another group write a synopsis of the top ten programs. Distribute a copy of the synopsis to each student. Have students watch as many of the programs as possible, rating each one using a simple scale (e.g., good, fair, poor). Have another group of students summarize the results of the class ratings and distribute a Guide for Viewing for the class to read.

**5. Delving Deeper:** Encourage depth of knowledge with older students by having them select an author or artist to read about. Then have them find other media about the person, including short stories, films, or videos. Ask students to provide a report detailing the facts about the person's life and draw inferences about them from their reading. Have them answer these questions: How is the author's life reflected in his or her work? How might the person's life be different today or at another time in history?

# Math

Low achievement in mathematics is less common than low achievement in reading, but problems with computation and analytical reasoning are major areas of learning difficulties. The following activities have been used to help students with learning disabilities in mathematics.

1. **Cues:** To reduce distractions and improve accuracy, provide cues and organizers to focus attention. For example, draw squares on worksheets and place math problems in them. This helps students with learning disabilities keep track of their progress and find their place a little easier. Some teachers also use answer blocks and other cues.

2. **Miniassignments:** Modify assignments to focus attention and reduce distraction. If students are reluctant to complete worksheets, reduce the number of problems on the page and provide several smaller assignments with breaks in between. For example, break a 20-problem worksheet into four miniassignments of 5 problems each.

3. **Accuracy Boosters:** To increase accuracy, provide multiple opportunities for success. Define **mastery** as achieving 100 percent correct after being told a previous attempt has errors. Have students try to achieve mastery with less than three retries.

4. **Manipulatives:** Use manipulatives to improve knowledge of basic facts. Beans, blocks, game chips, stickers, paper clips, and other small objects help students learn relationships between numbers and what they mean.

5. **Real-Life Applications:** Make math meaningful by using real-life problems and applications. Set up a classroom checking account and use it to help students with learning disabilities learn about money and related math (e.g., adding and subtracting credits and debits). Have students write checks to use in a classroom store.

6. **Clues:** To improve problem solving, teach basic concepts and have students practice using them. Teach students to look for clues in word problems, such as that the words *sum, all together,* and *plus* mean the problem requires addition. The words *spent, remains, left,* and *lost* are used frequently in subtraction problems.

7. **Simple Structures:** Improve performance by simplifying structure and content. Solving word problems is difficult when the vocabulary and writing style are above a student's reading level. Reducing the number of words in sentences from 15 to 5 can make the difference. You can also reduce the reading level by changing words like *remainder* to *how many left.*

8. **Activities:** Students with learning disabilities at all grade levels often report that they "hate" math. To improve interest and motivation, use activities like the one in *Figure 6.2* to keep students interested in math calculations and their applications.

# Written Language

Many students experience difficulties with written expression. The following activities can help students with learning disabilities achieve more skill in writing.

1. **Quantity Counts:** Focus on quantity before quality in written work. Students with learning disabilities often produce minimal amounts of written work or produce work with a large numbers of grammatical errors. Encouraging students to write as much as possible without concern for errors improves quantity, and from there you can work on quality.

2. **Checklists:** Use checklists to guide students before they write. Many students either do not know the features that go

**Figure 6.2**   Left-Right Addition (A Tricky Way to Add)

| 53 | Start with the first number at the top of the left- |
|---|---|
| 17 | hand column and call it by its "tens name" (50). |
| 24 | Add each number in the left-hand column to each |
| +19 | preceding number using the "tens names" and |
| 113 | continue down the ones column. |
| $(50 + 10 = 60 + 20 = 80 + 10 = 90 + 3 = 93 + 7 = 100 + 4 = 104 + 9 = 113)$ | |

into well-written work or simply fail to attend to the mechanics of writing. Giving students a checklist to use to evaluate their writing can improve the overall quality of their work. Decide what features are important. For example, some teachers are concerned about form as well as content. They want written products to reflect appropriate use of headings, references, and style. Others are more concerned about the visual appearance of written work (e.g., absence of unnecessary marks, clean erasures, and word or page limits). Whatever your focus, let students know, and help them evaluate their work before turning it in.

**3. Self-Evaluation:** Teach specific skills and have students monitor their written work. Teach composition skills (e.g., use of action words, action helpers, or describing words) in teacher-guided practice lessons, then have students evaluate their own writing (e.g., Did I use action words? Can I use more describing words? Did I tell how the action was done?).

**4. Familiar Words:** Practicing familiar words improves spelling overall. Teach students to think of familiar words as they try to spell a new word. Use common sight words that have at least five rhyming words and a similar spelling pattern as targeted spelling vocabulary (e.g., *big: pig, rig, jig, dig,* and *fig*). Have students read the rhyming words and teach them that when words rhyme, the last parts are often spelled the same. Give spelling tests using the rhyming words to improve students' confidence.

**5. Software:** Many teachers report that writing is easier for students with learning disabilities when they use word processing software. Students are more receptive to revising their work, and proofreading, editing, and spell-checking are easier. Some programs even guide students through the entire writing process, from brainstorming through revision. Desktop publishing software, which allows students to create newsletters and other in-class publications, can also boost motivation to produce a quality final product.

**6. Timed Exercises:** Build confidence by encouraging students to write as many words as they can as a brief, timed exercise that isn't graded for content or mechanics (spelling, grammar, etc.). Provide an option that the words can be related, but don't require it. Provide another option that the words can be in sentence form, but don't require it. At the end of the time period, count the number of words written and record the performance on a graph. Repeat the activity on subsequent days and encourage students to improve their writing by producing more words, by writing more correctly spelled words, by writing more complete sentences, or by writing about a topic.

# IMPROVING CLASSROOM BEHAVIOR

Inappropriate behavior is not a primary characteristic of students with learning disabilities, but work habits that interfere with productive academic performance can still be an issue. Many years of school failure often result in limited self-management and study skills, so it is important to address these areas.

## Work Habits

Given an opportunity to complete a school assignment, many students with learning disabilities respond with statements or actions that do not result in completion of the task. Task avoidance and nonattention can be improved by the following activities.

**1. Random Checks:** To focus and maintain attention, use random monitoring checks. Set an inexpensive kitchen timer to go off at randomly selected amounts of time. Reward students who are working when the timer sounds. An alternative is to play an audiotape that beeps at randomly selected time intervals. The tones are signals to check student work habits. Because they occur randomly, many students work constantly when the tape player or timer is on.

**2. Rewards:** To improve attention, reward students who are attending. Before distributing an independent assignment to the class, jot down several times to stop and pass out rewards to students who are working appropriately. Set the times at random rather than fixed intervals (e.g., 10:35, 10:41, 10:55 rather than 10:35, 10:45, 10:55). Start with small time intervals and gradually increase them as student behaviors improve.

**3. Self-Monitoring:** Use self-monitoring to improve attention. Prepare a tape-recorded sequence of tones spaced at intervals selected according to naturally-occurring levels of attention for the target student (e.g., 35 seconds, 45 seconds, 38 seconds or 2 minutes, 3 minutes, 4 minutes). When the tone sounds on the tape, have the students self-monitor using a checklist (see *Figure 6.3*). Reward improvements in attending that result from self-monitoring.

**4. Cues:** Use cues to reduce distractibility. Place written or pictorial cues (e.g., "start here" or "continue working after a brief rest") at appropriate places on a worksheet to help students with learning disabilities focus their attention and improve their behavior.

**5. Reward Classmates:** To reduce inappropriate behavior, reward appropriate behaviors. Keep track of specific behaviors used by a target student to avoid doing work (e.g., sharpening pencils, going to the restroom, staring out the window). Reward other class members when the target student is exhibiting task avoidance. By observing that task avoidance resulted in the loss of something positive, many students try to control their behavior in the future.

**Figure 6.3**   Was I Paying Attention?

*Morning*

| 1 _____ | 2 _____ | 3 _____ | 4 _____ | 5 _____ | |
|---|---|---|---|---|---|
| 6 _____ | 7 _____ | 8 _____ | 9 _____ | 10 _____ | of 10 = ___% |

| 1 _____ | 2 _____ | 3 _____ | 4 _____ | 5 _____ | |
|---|---|---|---|---|---|
| 6 _____ | 7 _____ | 8 _____ | 9 _____ | 10 _____ | of 10 = ___% |

*Afternoon*

| 1 _____ | 2 _____ | 3 _____ | 4 _____ | 5 _____ | |
|---|---|---|---|---|---|
| 6 _____ | 7 _____ | 8 _____ | 9 _____ | 10 _____ | of 10 = ___% |

| 1 _____ | 2 _____ | 3 _____ | 4 _____ | 5 _____ | |
|---|---|---|---|---|---|
| 6 _____ | 7 _____ | 8 _____ | 9 _____ | 10 _____ | of 10 = ___% |

**6. Daily Reports:** Use daily report cards to reduce inappropriate behavior. Inform parents that their children will be bringing a report card home each day. Have parents call for a verbal report if the student loses the written report on any day. Keep track of inappropriate behaviors (e.g., nonattention) as well as appropriate behaviors (e.g., time on task). Note improvements on graphs in the classroom and at home.

# Study Skills

Many students with learning disabilities don't use study time effectively. They may be disorganized, fail to listen carefully to directions, or don't ask appropriate questions about assignments. Help students to study more effectively with the following activities.

1. **Time Budgets:** Teach students to budget their time. Divide class periods into shorter time frames and help students make a list of tasks to be finished during each shorter time frame. Encourage students to develop their own schedules, and keep track of improvements in grades and classroom behavior on a classroom chart.

2. **Signals:** Provide students with signals to gain your attention. Some students have not learned positive

strategies for asking for help, so they don't bother to ask. Give students a small "help" sign that they can flash. Encourage students to personalize their signs—they'll be more likely to use them.

3. **Alternative Solutions:** Practice and discuss appropriate school behavior. Select a school situation related to studying (e.g., forgetting an assignment) and discuss the worst thing that a student can do if it happens. Have other students generate better solutions, and keep track of efforts to practice them.

4. **Clear Instructions:** Use care when giving instructions. Clearly and concisely state directions for assignments. Have students tell you the expected behavior before beginning their work.

5. **Organization:** Teach students to organize. Show them how to set up an assignment pad and notebook in the ways that are most efficient. Periodically check notebooks and assignment pads, and provide remedial instruction as needed. Don't assume that students with learning disabilities have acquired these skills on their own or that they will learn them from one instructional session.

6. **Group Projects:** Group students to encourage completion of assignments. Have students work together on a project and only accept completed work when all group members have finished their assignments. Encourage students in a group to share effective work habits and study skills.

## Bringing Learning to Life: Homework Buddies Help Mark Build Study Skills

Mark always had problems remembering assignments and completing homework on time. He was not the only one in his class who had this problem. His teachers decided to do something about it. They divided the class into groups of five. One of the students was assigned to be team leader each day of the week. Near the end of each school day, the teachers called on the team leaders to contact their group members and review homework assignments and progress on long-range projects (e.g., upcoming book reports, science fair projects). They used the simple checklist that follows to keep track. While Mark didn't always complete all of his homework, he did improve. He also enjoyed being part of the team and serving as team leader at least once a week.

**Homework Check**

Week of: _____     Team Name: _____

Team Members: _____

(Put initials in the spaces provided after homework check has been made)

| Monday | | | | | |
|---|---|---|---|---|---|
| Tuesday | | | | | |
| Wednesday | | | | | |
| Thursday | | | | | |
| Friday | | | | | |

# IMPROVING SOCIAL RELATIONS

Many students with learning disabilities have difficulty interacting with classmates. They are not as effective as their peers in initiating and maintaining appropriate social relations. The problems often result from the students' behaviors as well as from the attitudes of others toward them. Use the following activities to improve social relations of students with learning disabilities.

**1. Diversity:** Change attitudes with information. Words and actions provide a model for student behavior. Information about learning disabilities should be shared with students. Do not provide excuses for inappropriate behavior or encourage a sense of helplessness in students who are exceptional. Rather, encourage all students to value diversity and accept each other as individuals with strengths and weaknesses.

**2. Alternative Communication:** Provide alternative means for communicating. Some students with learning disabilities resist classroom discussions and interpersonal interactions because they are afraid of failure. Overcome this resistance by providing variety in the ways students can communicate. For example, students can talk into tape recorders about their problems rather than telling you face-to-face. Or students can keep interactive diaries with you or with classmates.

**3. Pairs:** Initiate group activities to foster socialization. Pair a withdrawn student with a more outgoing one and administer a group spelling test. Have a rule that each group member (initially two students) must spell at least one word on the test. Gradually increase the size of the group and the amount of interaction required by each member.

**4. Keeper:** Encourage interaction with structured activity. Arrange for the socially isolated student to be the keeper of a desirable classroom item (e.g., a favorite free-time game). Students who want to use the item must interact with the isolated student when they want to use it.

**5. Models:** Demonstrate and reward appropriate behavior. Appropriate social interaction skills can be taught to withdrawn students by having classmates demonstrate the behaviors. This is best accomplished by arranging for the behavior to be modeled and rewarded in the presence of the isolated student.

**6. Inclusive Activities:** Provide opportunities for varied social activities. Active participation of students in daily activities can improve interpersonal relations. Identify skills, hobbies, general interests, and individual experiences of all students. (They are usually eager to share them.) Plan group activities so that isolated as well as popular students are involved.

**7. Progress Reports:** Keep track of improvements in interaction skills, and send progress reports home on a regular basis.

**8. Sharing Information:** Highlight similarities and differences among students. Sharing information on strengths and weaknesses helps all students. Many of the characteristics of students with learning disabilities are similar to the characteristics of other students in the classroom. Differences are only obstacles if students and teachers make them such.

# 7

## *What Should Every Teacher Know About Learning Disabilities and ADHD?*

Much professional and parental attention has been focused on problems associated with inattention and hyperactivity. **Attention deficit hyperactivity disorder (ADHD)** is a disorder in which a student shows developmentally inappropriate degrees of inattention, impulsiveness, and hyperactivity. Associated features include low self-esteem, mood instability, low frustration tolerance, academic underachievement, problems with social relationships, and temper tantrums. ADHD is common, occurring in as many as 3 percent of children not currently classified and receiving special education.

## DEFINITIONS OF ADHD

Because characteristics of ADHD (e.g., attention problems, hyperactivity, or impulsivity) are also found in students with learning disabilities, recent professional concern has turned toward differentiating learning disabilities from ADHD, but little progress has been made. Students with ADHD receive special education services under Section 504 of the Rehabilitation Act (1973), but there is no federal category or definition for ADHD. The most widely accepted definitions appear in the *Diagnostic and Statistical Manual for Mental Disorders (DSM)* of the American Psychiatric Association (APA). The first set of characteristics that has become known as ADHD appeared in *DSM-II* and was called Hyperkinetic Reaction to Childhood (APA, 1968).

In *DSM-III*, 14 characteristics were organized into three groups: inattention, impulsivity, and hyperactivity (APA, 1980). This received considerable criticism because of the complexity created for professionals trying to differentiate among them. This led to a single list of 14 characteristics being associated with ADHD in *DSM-III-R* (APA, 1987), paving the way for the latest efforts to define ADHD in *DSM-IV* (McBurnett, Lahey, & Pfiffner, 1993).

Characteristics associated with ADHD are similar to those associated with learning disabilities (see *Table 7.1*). For example,

**Table 7.1**   Criteria for Attention Deficit Hyperactivity Disorder (ADHD)

---

**A. Either 1 or 2 must be present:**

*1. Inattention*

At least six of the following symptoms of inattention have persisted for at least six months to a degree that is maladaptive and inconsistent with developmental level.

    (a) Often fails to give close attention to details or makes careless mistakes in schoolwork, work, or other activities

    (b) Often has difficulty sustaining attention in tasks or play activities

    (c) Often does not seem to listen to what is being said

    (d) Often does not follow through on instruction and fails to finish schoolwork, chores, or duties in the workplace (not due to oppositional behavior or failure to understand instructions)

    (e) Often has difficulties organizing tasks and activities

    (f) Often avoids or strongly dislikes tasks that require sustained mental effort, such as schoolwork or homework

---

**Table 7.1** (Continued)

    (g) Often loses things necessary for tasks or activities (e.g., school assignments, pencils, books, tools, or toys)

    (h) Is often easily distracted by extraneous stimuli

    (i) Is often forgetful in daily activities

*2. Hyperactivity-Impulsivity*

At least six of the following symptoms of hyperactivity-impulsivity have persisted for at least six months to a degree that is maladaptive and inconsistent with developmental level.

*Hyperactivity*

    (a) Often fidgets with hands or feet or squirms in seat

    (b) Leaves seat in classroom or in other situations in which remaining seated is expected

    (c) Often runs about or climbs excessively in situations where it is inappropriate (in adolescents or adults, may be limited to subjective feelings of restlessness)

    (d) Often has difficulty playing or engaging in leisure activities quietly

    (e) Often talks excessively

    (f) Often acts as if "driven by a motor" and cannot remain still

*Impulsivity*

    (g) Often blurts out answers to questions before questions have been completed

    (h) Often has difficulty waiting in lines or awaiting turns in games or group situations

    (i) Often interrupts or intrudes on others

**B. Onset is no later than 7 years of age.**

**C. Symptoms must be present in two or more situations (e.g., at school, work, and at home).**

**D. The disturbance causes clinically significant distress or impairment in social, academic, or occupational functioning.**

**E. The symptoms do not occur exclusively during the course of other disorders.**

*Source:* Task Force on *DSM-IV* (1993).

inattention, hyperactivity, and impulsivity are key behavioral characteristics associated with learning disabilities, and "clinically significant distress or impairment in academic functioning" is analogous to "significant discrepancy between ability and achievement" (Task Force on *DSM-IV*, 1993, p. 81). Moreover, interventions prescribed for students with ADHD are often used with students with learning disabilities (e.g., training or shaping appropriate behaviors, reducing inappropriate behaviors, creating stimulating learning tasks, and using varied instructional activities).

# PRINCIPLES OF REMEDIATION

Professionals concerned with students with ADHD offer the following principles of remediation for inattention, excessive activity, and impulsivity (CHADD, 1992).

## Inattention

1. Decrease the length of the task.
   - Break one task into smaller parts to be completed at different times.
   - Give two tasks, with a preferred task to be completed after the less preferred task.
   - Give fewer spelling words or math problems.
   - Use fewer words in explaining tasks (concise and global verbal directions).
   - Use distributed practice for rote tasks rather than mass practice.

2. Make tasks interesting.
   - Allow student to work with partners, in small groups, or in centers.
   - Alternate high- and low-interest tasks.
   - Use overhead projector when lecturing.
   - Allow student to sit closer to the teacher.

3. Increase novelty—especially into later time periods of longer tasks.
   - Make a game out of checking work.
   - Use games to overlearn rote material.

## Excessive Activity

1. Do not attempt to reduce activity, but channel it into acceptable avenues.

2. Encourage directed movement in classrooms that is not disruptive. Allow standing during seatwork, especially during end of task.

3. Use activity as reward. Give special activities (running an errand, cleaning the board, organizing teacher's desk, arranging chairs) as individual rewards for improvement.

4. Use active responses in instruction. Use teaching activities that encourage active responding (talking, moving, organizing, working at the board).

5. Encourage daily writing, painting, and so forth.

6. Teach student to ask questions that are on the topic.

## Impulsivity

1. Give the student substitute verbal or motor responses to make while waiting and, where possible, encourage daydreaming or planning while waiting.

2. Instruct the student on how to continue on easier parts of a task (or do a substitute task) while waiting for help.

3. Have the student underline or rewrite the directions before beginning, or give the student markers or colored pencils to underline the directions and relevant information.

4. Encourage doodling or play with clay, paper clips, and pipe cleaners while waiting or listening to instruction.

5. Encourage note taking (even just cue words).

Teachers are likely to have at least one student whose behavior is characterized by symptoms associated with inattention, hyperactivity, or impulsivity. Sometimes the students are identified with specific learning disabilities or other conditions (e.g., ADHD). Sometimes students are not classified at all.

Paying attention, listening, following directions, sitting still, playing quietly, waiting, concentrating, and remembering are difficult for many students, especially when doing them competes with other more interesting things to do (as far as they are concerned). Take heart, for while there's plenty of interest and attention provided these students and their problems, there's not much mystery here. Effective teaching is effective teaching. Stimulating, active lessons go a long way in focusing the attention and controlling the activity of *many* of these students.

# 8

# What Trends and Issues Influence How We Teach Students With Learning Disabilities?

I t has always been difficult for professionals to differentiate learning disabilities from other conditions. By defining learning disabilities as a specific condition, professionals hoped to reduce problems. But since the beginning of the field of learning disabilities in 1963, it has been difficult to arrive at a widely accepted definition. In 1977, federal officials specified a definition that focused on underlying psychological processing disorders and on discrepancies between abilities and achievement. They were met with the following criticisms:

All of us have "imperfect abilities" in some areas and thus can be considered learning disabled.

Underlying psychological processing disorders (e.g., figure-ground discrimination, visual perception, memory) are difficult to assess. Some professionals do not believe they are appropriate targets for instruction.

People have trouble differentiating students with learning disabilities from those with emotional disturbance, mental retardation, or ADHD. Learning disabilities can coexist with other problems.

Discrepancies between ability and achievement scores are technically inadequate, simplistic, misleading (leading to a focus on single areas of disability), and systematically biased against students who earn low scores on intelligence tests.

Professionals can't agree on the magnitude of discrepancy necessary for identification with specific learning disabilities.

# A CHANGING DEFINITION

Criticism of the federal definition led to formation of the National Joint Committee for Learning Disabilities (NJCLD), an organization made up of representatives from the major professional organizations in the field. In 1981, NJCLD proposed a new definition of learning disabilities that stressed the general nature of problems grouped under the term. In 1984, the Association for Children and Adults with Learning Disabilities adopted a definition that broadened the scope of the problem beyond academics. More recently, another study group, appointed by the National Institutes of Health, proposed to Congress a new definition of learning disabilities that extends it to the area of social skills and makes an effort to express the relationship between learning disabilities and ADHD.

Professionals are not yet united on whether to include process disorders, socioenvironmental influences, or attention deficit disorders in the definition of learning disabilities. And professionals are not united in their belief or stance on whether or not students who have other kinds of conditions, such as mental retardation, emotional disturbance, blindness, or giftedness, can also be included in the category of specific learning disabilities. Some have tried to address this lack of unity by indicating that there may be more than one type of learning disability.

# SUBTYPES OF LEARNING DISABILITIES

In recent definitions, *learning disabilities* is considered an umbrella term. It is referred to as a heterogeneous condition or a generic term. Some now propose specific subtypes of students with learning disabilities. For example, Chalfant and Kirk (1984) describe two kinds of students: those with *academic* learning disabilities, like disabilities in reading, arithmetic, spelling, and writing; and those with *developmental* learning disabilities, which are disorders or dysfunctions in the processes or abilities necessary to acquiring academic skills. Developmental learning disabilities include deficits or disorders in attention, memory, perceptual-motor functioning, perception, thinking, or language.

James McKinney (1984) described seven subtypes of problem areas of students with learning disabilities. The first five subtypes are

1. Attention deficits

2. Conduct problems

3. Withdrawn behavior

4. Low positive behavior

5. Global behavior problems.

McKinney's (1984) final two subtypes relate to students who behave normally but have elevated scores on measures of specific personality traits. Such subtyping is a relatively arbitrary process. We have found it difficult to use in any practical way, for instance in planning specific instructional interventions.

# DEFINITIONS VARY BY STATE

Definitions for specific learning disabilities vary from state to state. Sometimes eligibility criteria vary among school districts within states as well. This means that a student may receive special education services in one district, then move to another and not be eligible anymore. Finding the best definition of *learning disability* is one of the challenges that continue to face professionals. Developing appropriate and effective programs for adults with learning disabilities is another.

# TRANSITION QUESTIONS

Information on what happens to students with learning disabilities after school is relatively sparse (how many attend college, find successful employment, are successful in transition to adulthood, etc.). This area is becoming increasingly important as the large number of students classified as learning disabled during the 1980s and 1990s age out of school. Studies show that adults with learning disabilities are often concerned about problems with social and occupational skills that are taken for granted by people who have been successful in school. Often they report anxiety about their jobs and believe they need to improve their interpersonal relations, work harder and longer, and recognize their limitations more than their colleagues. As the large numbers of students with learning disabilities grow up and leave school, support services for transition and the world of work will continue to grow in importance.

# 9

# *Learning Disabilities in Perspective*

There are many competing viewpoints on how to define learning disabilities and about who is learning disabled. At the same time, there is agreement that some students do not perform as well as they might in school. There is reason to believe that there may be internal causes of difficulty and that, in addition to learning disabilities, students can have other disorders and need special education services. The debate about how best to define and identify students with learning disabilities continues in the professional literature, and there is some variability among states in the numbers of students identified and served in this category. While very many traits and characteristics have been attributed to students with learning disabilities, and students who are identified as learning disabled do demonstrate many of these, there are no characteristics that are universal and specific to the condition.

Many of the students who experience significant learning disabilities or disorders *do* demonstrate many of the cognitive characteristics we have described. Yet not all students who exhibit learning disabilities show these characteristics. And many students who have no difficulty whatsoever learning in school (students considered "normal") evidence the characteristics as well. Many students who are considered mentally retarded, emotionally disturbed, speech and language impaired, deaf, blind, or otherwise disabled show the same characteristics. Most characteristics associated with poor performance in school are not **universal** (evidenced by *everyone* who is said to be learning disabled) or **specific** (evidenced *only* by students who are said to be learning disabled). Use of liberal eligibility criteria sometimes leads to faulty reasoning:

Students with learning disabilities have memory problems.

McGillicuddy has memory problems.

McGillicuddy is a student with learning disabilities.

By the same token, someone might offer the following reasoning:

Dogs like steak.

You like steak.

You are a dog.

Inappropriate labeling—created by misapplication of an overly simplified identification process and liberal eligibility criteria—remains a fundamental concern for professionals in special education. Recall that the number of students in the learning disabilities category increased by more than 100 percent since 1977. And while growth at similar levels is unlikely in the future, you can expect to find students with learning disabilities at every grade level in any school where you teach.

# 10

## *What Have We Learned?*

As you complete your study of teaching students with learning disabilities, it may be helpful to review what you have learned. To help you check your understanding, we have listed the key points and key vocabulary for you to review. We have included the Self-Assessment again so you can compare what you know now with what you knew as you began your study. Finally, we provide a few topics for you to think about and some activities for you to do on your own.

## KEY POINTS

▣ Learning disabilities is the newest, most rapidly growing area in special education.

▣ The term *learning disability* was first used in 1963 to describe students having difficulties in school but with no other obvious disability.

▣ Although there is no single, universally accepted definition, students with learning disabilities exhibit significant academic difficulties that cannot be attributed to any other special education condition. They need extra assistance to be successful in school.

▣ A variety of characteristics have been identified in students with learning disabilities, but the most common is a specific and significant discrepancy between ability and achievement in at least one area of academic functioning.

▣ Learning disabilities are sometimes called hidden problems because students with them often have strengths that mask weaknesses in specific areas.

▣ Students with ADHD exhibit many of the same characteristics as students with learning disabilities, and many of the interventions used with them are appropriate for other students as well.

▣ Many types of instructional activities are used by teachers and other professionals to help these students be successful in school and later life.

# Key Vocabulary

**Analytical programs** refer to programs developed based on an instructional approach where readers are taught a systematic method of decoding words.

**Attention Deficit Hyperactivity Disorder (ADHD)** is a disorder in which a student shows developmentally inappropriate degrees of inattention, impulsiveness, and hyperactivity.

**Basic skills** include the ability to listen, think, and speak as well as read, write, spell, and do mathematical calculations.

**Cues** refer to actions taken by teachers to help pupils reduce distractions and to focus attention.

**Discrepancy** refers to the difference between expected and actual achievement.

**Functional academic assessment** is a process used to identify the extent to which evidence-based principles of effective instruction are used to teach the student.

**Functional behavioral assessment** is a framework used by assessors to identify factors that cause or support the occurrence of a behavior.

**Hyperactivity-impulsivity** refers to behaviors of excessive motor activity and impulsive responding.

**Inattention** refers to behaviors related to having difficulty paying attention.

**Learning disability** is a disorder in one or more of the basic psychological processes involved in understanding or in using language; it may manifest itself in an imperfect ability to listen, think, speak, read, write, spell, or do mathematical calculations. It is often identified by a discrepancy between expected and actual achievement. It is also called *specific learning disability*.

**Minitest** is a short exercise for students to practice a specific skill.

**Phonetic cues** are a technique of decoding words by looking for cues applying phonetic rules.

**Process disorders** refer to problems in internal processes, such as problems remembering things, discriminating between visual or auditory perceptions, and developing and using cognitive strategies.

**Thematic units** are instructional units designed around a theme to encourage the integration of various areas of instruction.

**Whole language program** refers to programs based on an instructional approach where students are taught reading skills by actually using them rather than by learning and practicing word-recognition skills.

# Self-Assessment 2

After you complete this book, check your knowledge and understanding of the content covered. Choose the best answer for each of the following questions.

1. Which one of the following methods would NOT be a means of identifying students with learning disabilities?

   a. Showing that a child demonstrates a developmental delay

   b. Providing evidence that a child has a process disorder

   c. Providing evidence that a child has not responded to generally effective instruction

   d. Demonstrating that a child presents a discrepancy between academic achievement and intellectual ability

2. The definition of children with learning disabilities includes those _____ .

   a. with mental retardation

   b. who have writing difficulties

   c. with severe visual impairment

   d. who come from disadvantaged families

3. From 1990 to 2003, what was the increase in the number of school-aged children identified with learning disabilities?

   a. 30%

   b. 40%

   c. 50%

   d. 60%

4. What is the problem with assessing for processing disorders as a basis for identifying children with learning disorders?

   a. It is time consuming.

   b. Children may be negatively affected by such tests.

   c. The measurements of such disorders are inadequate.

   d. The cost is beyond the means of the average-income family.

5. Using curriculum-based measures, teachers are able to identify children whose _____ and rate of performance are below those of their classmates.

   a. Level

   b. Height

   c. Quality

   d. Frequency

6. What kind of information is gathered from a functional behavioral assessment?

   a. The specific skills that a student is able to perform

   b. The factors that cause the occurrence of a behavior

   c. The effectiveness of a behavior intervention program

   d. The level at which a child is functioning in the classroom

7. In _____ programs, students are taught reading skills by actually using them, together with other communication skills.

   a. Analytical

   b. Comprehensive

c. Structured

d. Whole language

8. One way to avoid the use of liberal eligibility criteria in the identification of learning disabilities is to ensure that a characteristic used in the criteria is both _____ and specific.

    a. Holistic

    b. Objective

    c. Observable

    d. Universal

9. _____ activities, such as getting children to talk about their hobbies, encourage students with disabilities to be integrated in a class.

    a. Alternative communication

    b. Cooperative

    c. Inclusive

    d. Socializing

10. Which one of the following traits is NOT considered a primary feature in the criteria for identifying children for ADHD?

    a. Adaptability

    b. Hyperactivity

    c. Impulsivity

    d. Inattention

# REFLECTION

After you answer the multiple-choice questions, think about how you would answer the following questions:

- Define specific learning disabilities as stated in the 1997 reauthorization of IDEA. Give three problems associated with the definition.
- There has been a rapid growth in the number of students identified with specific learning disabilities. What do you think are some reasons for this phenomenon?
- Briefly describe one strategy you would use to help a child

    a. With reading difficulties

    b. Who lacks study skills

    c. Who has difficulty paying attention in class

# Answer Key for Self-Assessments

1.  a

2.  b

3.  a

4.  c

5.  a

6.  b

7.  d

8.  d

9.  c

10. a

# On Your Own

☑ Visit a professor who teaches coursework in the area of learning disabilities. Obtain answers to the following questions:

- What definition is used by school districts for identifying students with learning disabilities in your state?

- How many students with learning disabilities are in your state?

- What special courses do teachers being certified in learning disabilities take?

- What are some specific activities that teachers use to remediate reading problems of students with learning disabilities?

- What are some specific activities that teachers use to remediate problems with math of students with learning disabilities?

- What are some specific activities that teachers use to remediate language problems of students with learning disabilities?

☑ Select a journal that focuses on students with learning disabilities. Browse the most recent issues in your library. Find at least three articles that describe specific teaching activities that you could use to improve the reading skills of students with learning disabilities. Find at least three articles that describe specific teaching activities that you could use to improve the mathematics skills of students with learning disabilities. Summarize each activity.

☑ Contact a local, state, or national organization that focuses on people with learning disabilities. Identify the purpose of the organization, its membership, and its services.

☑ Look in the Yellow Pages of your local phone book for people or agencies that provide afterschool tutoring. Call several and ask about the kinds of services they provide and how they work with teachers to meet the needs of students with learning disabilities and their families.

☑ Imagine that you are a teacher with several students with learning disabilities in your classroom. What decisions would you have to make to help these students be successful? What instructional approaches would be appropriate for working with them? What specific activities would you use to modify a lesson you were teaching to your class on fractions?

☑ Prepare a table illustrating the numbers of students with specific learning disabilities in your state and a few neighboring states. Compare the figures and come up with three reasons for any variation that you identify.

# *Resources*

## BOOKS

Dwyer, K. M. (1991). *What do you mean I have a learning disability?* New York: Walker. A photographic essay told by a ten-year-old who thinks he is stupid because he is forgetful, awkward, and having problems in school. This is an excellent book for elementary school students.

Lerner, J. (2003). *Learning disabilities: Theories, diagnosis, and teaching strategies* (9th ed.). Boston: Houghton Mifflin. This overview of learning disabilities focuses on the assessment and teaching process and includes theoretical perspectives and instructional strategies.

Marek, M. (1988). *Different, not dumb.* New York: Watts. Second grader Mike has reading problems because of a learning disability. Elementary school students will enjoy this book.

## JOURNALS AND ARTICLES

*Intervention in School and Clinic (ISC).* This interdisciplinary journal is directed to an international audience of teachers, parents, educational therapists, and specialists who deal with the day-to-day aspects of special and remedial education. Articles focus on specific intervention approaches and activities. ISC, Pro-Ed Publications, 8700 Shoal Creek Blvd, Austin, TX 78757–6897.

*Journal of Learning Disabilities (JLD).* This multidisciplinary journal contains articles on practice, research, and theory related to learning disabilities. It includes reports of research, opinion papers, case reports, and discussions of issues. Sharon Vaughn, Editor-in-Chief, JLD, Pro-Ed Publications, 8700 Shoal Creek Blvd, Austin, TX 78757–6897.

*Learning Disabilities Quarterly (LDQ).* This publication of the Council for Learning Disabilities includes educational articles with an applied focus. The main emphasis is on learning disabilities rather than on topics or studies that incidentally use students with learning disabilities or only indirectly relate to the field of learning disabilities. Council for Learning Disabilities, P.O. Box 40303 Overland Park, KS 66204.

*Learning Disabilities Research & Practice (LDRP).* The Division for Learning Disabilities publishes this journal to provide a forum for current research and to improve service to individuals with learning disabilities. Council for Exceptional Children, 1110 North Glebe Road, Arlington, VA 22201–5704.

# ORGANIZATIONS

## *Children With Attention Deficit Disorders (CHADD)*

CHADD is the most comprehensive source of up-to-date information on ADD in the United States. CHADD, 499 NW 70th Avenue, Suite 308, Plantation, FL 33317.

## *Council for Learning Disabilities (CLD)*

Founded in 1968 as a division of the Council for Exceptional Children (CEC), CLD became an independent organization in 1982 to become a multidisciplinary group. CLD promotes the exchange of ideas through an annual conference, news releases, and *Learning Disabilities Quarterly.* CLD, P.O. Box 40303, Overland Park, KS 66204.

## Division for Learning Disabilities (DLD)

Founded in 1982, DLD is concerned primarily with educational issues. It provides advocacy, inservice training, and regional and national conferences, as well as publishing *Learning Disabilities Research & Practice*. DLD, Council for Exceptional Children, 1100 North Glebe Road, Suite 300, Arlington, VA 22201.

## Learning Disabilities Association of America (LDA)

Founded in 1963, LDA is the largest organized group in the field of learning disabilities, with over 50,000 members. LDA is concerned primarily with parental issues and advocates for children with learning disabilities. They host an annual conference and publish professional publications. LDA, 4156 Library Road, Pittsburgh, PA 15234.

## National Attention Deficit Disorder Association (ADDA)

ADDA is a key information source for parents and professionals interested in ADD. They host meetings and publish professional publications. ADDA, P.O. Box 488, West Newbury, MA 01985.

## The Orton Dyslexia Society, Inc. (ODS)

Founded in 1949 in honor of Samuel T. Orton, a physician who studied diverse language disorders, ODS maintains a medical and educational focus that is broader than most other organizations related to learning disabilities. ODS publishes *Annals of Dyslexia* and *Perspectives on Dyslexia*. ODS, 724 York Road, Baltimore, MD 21204.

# References

American Psychiatric Association. (1968). *Diagnostic and statistical manual of mental disorders* (2nd ed.). Washington, DC: Author.

American Psychiatric Association. (1980). *Diagnostic and statistical manual of mental disorders* (3rd ed.). Washington, DC: Author.

American Psychiatric Association. (1987). *Diagnostic and statistical manual of mental disorders* (3rd ed., rev.). Washington, DC: Author.

CHADD. (1992, November/December). The teacher's challenge. The *CHADDer Box, 5*(7), 14–15.

Chalfant, J. C., & Kirk, S. A. (1984). *Academic and developmental learning disabilities.* Denver, CO: Love.

Education for All Handicapped Children Act, Pub. L. No. 94–142, 89 Stat. 773 (1975).

Fuchs, D., Mock, D., Morgan, P. L., & Young, C. L. (2003). Responsiveness-to-intervention: Definitions, evidence, and implications for the learning disabilities construct. *Learning Disabilities Research & Practice, 18*(3), 157–171.

Individuals With Disabilities Education Act, Pub. L. No. 101–476, 104 Stat. 1141 (1990).

McBurnett, K., Lahey, B. B., & Pfiffner, L. J. (1993). Diagnosis of attention deficit disorders in DSM-IV: Scientific basis and implications for education. *Exceptional Children, 60,* 108–117.

McKinney, J. D. (1984). The search for subtypes of specific learning disability. *Journal of Learning Disabilities, 17*(1), 43–50.

National Joint Committee on Learning Disabilities. (2002). *Specific learning disabilities: Finding common ground.* Washington, DC: U.S. Department of Education, Division of Research to Practice, Office of Special Education Programs.

Rehabilitation Act, Pub. L. No. 93–112, 87 Stat. 357 (1973).

Speece, D., Case, L. P., & Molloy, D. E. (2003). Responsiveness to general education instruction as the first gate in learning disabilities identification. *Learning Disabilities Research and Practice, 18*(3), 147–156.

Stahl, S. A., Osborn, J., & Lehr, F. (1990). *Beginning to read: Thinking and learning about print: A summary.* Champaign, IL: Center for the Study of Reading.

Task Force on *DSM-IV.* (1993). *DSM-IV Draft Criteria, 3-1-93.* (Available from American Psychiatric Press, Inc., 1400 K Street, N. W., Suite 1101, Washington, DC 20005).

U.S. Department of Education. (1997). Individuals With Disabilities Education Act: Final Regulations [§300.7 (c) (2)]. Washington, DC: Author.

U.S. Department of Education. (2001). *Twenty-third annual report to Congress on the implementation of the Individuals With Disabilities Education Act.* Washington, DC: U.S. Government Printing Office, Appendix AA2.

U.S. Department of Education. (2002). *Twenty-Fourth Annual Report to Congress on the implementation of the Individuals With Disabilities Education Act.* Washington, DC: U.S. Government Printing Office, Appendix AA3.

Ysseldyke, J., & Christenson, S. L. (2002). *Functional assessment of academic behavior: Creating successful learning environments.* Longmont, CO: Sopris West Educational Services.

# Index

*Note:* Numbers in **Bold** followed by a colon [:] denote the book number within which the page numbers are found.

AAMR (American Association on Mental Retardation), **12**:6, **12**:20–21, **12**:66
Ability training, **4**:39–40, **4**:62
Academic achievement, assessing, **3**:37–39
  achievement tests, **3**:37, **3**:77
  interviews, **3**:38–39
  observations, **3**:38
  portfolios, **3**:39
Academic engaged time, **3**:22–23, **3**:76
Academic learning disabilities, **9**:51
Academic time analysis, **3**:22–23, **3**:76
Acceleration or advancement, **13**:25–27, **13**:36–40, **13**:52
Acceptability, **3**:56–57
Accommodations
  defining, **3**:77
  for student with sensory disabilities, **7**:49–51
  in general education classrooms, **1**:21–22
  without patronization, **4**:14
  *See also* Instruction, adapting for students with special needs

Accountability, **3**:17, **3**:77
  outcomes-based, **3**:23, **6**:35
Acculturation, **3**:63, **3**:77
Achievement tests, **3**:37, **3**:77
Acting out, **3**:47
Active observation, **3**:29, **3**:77
Adams, C. M., **1**:35–36
Adaptive behavior, **3**:41–43, **3**:77
  defining, **12**:21
  environmental effects on, **3**:42–43
  mental retardation and, **12**:17, **12**:19–25, **12**:21 (tab)–23 (tab), **12**:45–49
Adaptive behavior scales, **3**:42, **12**:71
Adaptive devices, **8**:52, **8**:62–63
ADHD. *See* Attention deficit hyperactivity disorder
Adult literacy/lifelong learning, **5**:50, **6**:27–28
Advanced Placement (AP), **13**:26
Advocacy groups, **6**:11, **6**:12–13, **6**:44
Ahlgren, C., **12**:67
AIDS, **5**:10, **8**:12–13, **8**:58–59, **8**:63
Aim line, **4**:29, **4**:63
Alcohol-/drug-free schools, **6**:28–29
Algozzine, B., **4**:5, **6**:9, **12**:62
Alley, G., **4**:45

Allocation of funds,
    **6:**15, **6:**16–17, **6:**44
Allsop, J., **8:**49
Alternative living unit (ALU),
    **5:**31, **5:**54
Alternative-print format, **3:**71
Alternatives for recording
    answers, **3:**71
Amendments to the Education for
    All Handicapped Children Act,
    **2:**11 (tab)
Amendments to the Individuals
    With Disabilities Education
    Act, **2:**12 (tab), **2:**27–29
American Association on Mental
    Retardation (AAMR),
    **12:**6, **12:**11, **12:**18–19,
    **12:**20–21, **12:**66
American Asylum for the
    Education and Instruction
    of the Deaf, **2:**9–10
American Federation
    of Teachers, **6:**11
American Psychiatric
    Association, **9:**44
American Sign Language (ASL),
    **7:**40, **7:**59
American Speech-Language-
    Hearing Association
    (ASHA), **10:**10, **10:**35
Americans With Disabilities
    Act (ADA), **2:**12 (tab),
    **2:**26–27, **2:**54, **8:**49
Amplification systems, **4:**51, **7:**41
Analysis error, **3:**38, **3:**78
Analytical programs, **9:**27, **9:**56
Antia, S. D., **7:**26
Anxiety, **11:**18–22, **11:**46
AP (Advanced Placement), **13:**26
Apprenticeships programs,
    **5:**45, **5:**56
Appropriate education,
    **2:**42 (tab), **2:**46, **2:**54
ARC (Association for Retarded
    Citizens), **12:**66
Architectural accessibility, **2:**14, **2:**54
Articulation disorder,
    **10:**9–10, **10:**43

Asch, A., **7:**33–34
ASHA (American
    Speech-Language-Hearing
    Association), **10:**10, **10:**35
Assessment
    academic achievement, **3:**37–39
    alternatives for recording
        answers, **3:**71
    classroom, **3:**73–74
    curriculum-based,
        **3:**19–21, **3:**78, **9:**19
    data collection for, **3:**25–31
    defining, **3:**77
    ecobehavioral, **3:**22–23, **3:**78
    effects of, **3:**74
    error and, **3:**62–63
    formal, **3:**11
    functional academic,
        **9:**19, **9:**57
    functional behavioral, **9:**19, **9:**57,
        **11:**15–16, **11:**47
    instructional environments,
        **3:**23, **3:**77
    needs, **4:**41, **4:**64
    portfolios, **3:**26, **3:**39, **3:**80
    prereferral interventions, **3:**11
    psychoeducational, **3:**9, **3:**81
    psychological development,
        **3:**45–47
    skilled examiner for, **3:**59–61
    work-sample, **3:**26, **3:**81
    *See also* Assessment guidelines;
        Assessment practices; Data
        collection; Protection in
        evaluation procedures
Assessment,
    decision-making and
    accountability, **3:**17
    child-study team role in, **3:**12–15
    eligibility/entitlement, **3:**14–15
    exceptionality decisions, **3:**12
    instructional planning, **3:**15
    intervention assistance, **3:**10
    overview of, **3:**8 (tab)
    program evaluation, **3:**16–17
    progress evaluation, **3:**15–16
    psychoeducational assessment
        referral, **3:**9

screening decisions, **3:**7–10
special help/enrichment, **3:**10
special learning needs, **3:**13–14
Assessment guidelines, **3:**65–71
accommodation, **3:**71
environment, **3:**70–71
frequency, **3:**69
improving instruction, **3:**69
more than describing
problems, **3:**67–69
no one cause of school
problems, **3:**66
no right way to assess, **3:**66
variables, **3:**70
Assessment practices, **3:**17–24
curriculum-based assessment,
**3:**19–21
curriculum-based measurement,
**3:**21–22
instructional diagnosis, **3:**22
instructional
environments, **3:**23
outcomes-based accountability,
**3:**23
performance assessment, **3:**24
*See also* Reliability;
Representativeness; Validity
Assisted listening devices,
**7:**39 (tab), **7:**41, **7:**42
Assistive technologies,
**2:**26, **7:**13, **7:**52
Association for Retarded Citizens
(ARC), **12:**66
Asthma, **8:**9–10, **8:**11 (tab), **8:**63
Astigmatism, **7:**10, **7:**59
At risk student, **2:**24, **3:**8, **3:**9,
**5:**14–15, **6:**20, **13:**14
Ataxic cerebral palsy, **8:**24
Athetoid cerebral palsy, **8:**24
Attack strategy training,
**4:**40, **4:**63
Attention deficit
hyperactivity disorder
(ADHD), **2:**15, **8:**34
criteria for, **9:**44 (tab)–45 (tab)
defining, **9:**43–46, **9:**56
remediating, **9:**46–48
Audio aids, **7:**36 (tab)

Audiometer, **3:**40, **3:**77
Auditory acuity, **7:**19, **7:**59
Autism, **1:**15–16, **1:**40, **8:**17,
**8:**28–31, **8:**63
Automaticity, **4:**20, **4:**63
Auxiliary aids, **2:**14

Bain, J. D., **4:**5
Barnett, S., **5:**16
Barraga, N. C., **7:**8
Basic skills, **9:**56
Batshaw, M. L., **8:**22, **8:**47
*Beattie v. State Board of Education,*
**2:**36 (tab)
Behavior intervention plan, **11:**16,
**11:**46
Behavior therapy, **4:**38, **4:**63
Bennett, T., **3:**21
Berdine, W. H., **8:**46
Berrueta-Clement, J., **5:**16
Biklen, D., **6:**41
Bingo (game), **12:**40 (fig)
Blackhurst, A. E., **8:**46
Blackorby, J., **5:**24
Bland, L. C., **1:**35–36
Blindisms, **7:**14
Blindness, **1:**16
defining, **1:**40, **7:**8–9, **7:**59
*See also* Braille; Visual
impairments
Bloom, B., **4:**41
Books (resources)
assessment, **3:**91–92
communication
disorders, **10:**57
effective instruction, **4:**75–76
emotional disturbance, **11:**57–60
fundamentals of special
education, **1:**53
gifted and talented child,
**13:**63–64
learning disabilities, **9:**67
legal foundations, **2:**65–66
medical/physical/multiple
disabilities, **8:**75–80
mental retardation, **12:**81–84
public policy/school
reform, **6:**55

sensory disabilities, **7:**73–77
   transitions, **5:**65–67
Bounty hunting, **6:**17
Braille, **4:**52, **7:**10, **7:**13, **7:**15, **7:**16,
   **7:**34, **7:**35 (tab)
Braille display technology,
   **7:**37, **7:**59
Braille note-taking devices, **7:**38
Braille printers, **7:**37, **7:**59
Brailler, **4:**52, **4:**63
Brooks-Gunn, J., **5:**15
Brophy, J., **4:**13
Brown, F., **3:**62–63
Brown, L., **12:**55, **12:**67
*Brown v. Board of Education,*
   **2:**35, **2:**36 (tab), **2:**44
Bryant, B., **3:**37
Bureau of Indian Affairs,
   **6:**11, **6:**13
*Burlington School Committee*
   *v. Massachusetts Board of*
   *Education,* **2:**42 (tab), **2:**46–47
Byrnes, L. J., **7:**26

Callahan, C. M., **1:**35–36
Cameto, R., **5:**24
Cancer, **8:**11 (tab), **8:**63
Canes, for students with visual
   impairments, **4:**55
Carrow-Woolfolk, E., **10:**26
Carta, J., **3:**22, **4:**46
Carter, K., **7:**38
Cartwright, C., **4:**53
Cartwright, G., **4:**53
Case, L. P., **9:**17–18
Categorical programs,
   **1:**17, **6:**16, **6:**44
CCTV (closed-circuit television),
   **7:**35 (tab), **7:**36–37
CEC (Council for Exceptional
   Children), **12:**66
*Cefalu v. East Baton Rouge*
   *Parish School Board,*
   **2:**43 (tab)–44 (tab)
Center-based programs,
   **5:**13, **5:**14, **5:**54
Cerebral palsy, **8:**23–24, **8:**63
CHADD, **9:**46

Chadsey-Rusch, J., **5:**24
Chalfant, J. C., **9:**51
Chang, S. C., **7:**15
Child-find programs,
   **7:**30, **7:**59
Child-study team, **3:**12–15, **3:**77
Choate, J., **3:**21
Christenson, S. L., **3:**14, **3:**23
Citizens Concerned About
   Disability, **6:**11
Civil Rights Act, **2:**26
Clark, B., **4:**41
Classification
   changes in practices, **6:**8–9
   defining, **6:**44
Classroom amplification systems,
   **7:**41, **7:**51
Classroom assessment, **3:**73–74
Classwide peer tutoring,
   **4:**47, **4:**63
Client-centered therapy,
   **4:**43–44, **4:**63
Cloninger, C., **12:**59
Close-captioned television, **4:**51
Closed-circuit television (CCTV),
   **7:**35 (tab), **7:**36–37
Coefficient, reliability, **3:**50, **3:**81
Cognitive behavior modification,
   **4:**41, **4:**63
Cognitive mapping, **7:**34
Cognitive skills training,
   **4:**41, **4:**43
Cohen, H. J., **8:**13
Coleman, M. C., **11:**36
Coleman, M. R., **13:**11, **13:**45
Committee for Economic
   Development, **5:**14–15
Communication boards,
   **4:**50, **8:**41, **8:**63
Communication disorders
   academic characteristics
      of, **10:**14
   behavioral characteristics
      of, **10:**15
   cognitive characteristics
      of, **10:**13–14
   combating negative stereotypes
      about, **10:**37 (tab)–38

communication characteristics
of, **10**:15–16
defining, **10**:43
fluency problems, **10**:16
identifying, **10**:24–27
language disorders, **10**:10–11
language problems, **10**:16
phonology/morphology/
syntax problems, **10**:10–11
physical characteristics of,
**10**:14–15
pragmatics problems, **10**:11
pulling students from classroom,
**10**:36–37
semantics problems, **10**:11
speech disorders, **10**:9–10
team approach to providing
services, **10**:35–36
tips to improve communication,
**10**:38
voice problems, **10**:15
*See also* Communication
disorders, teaching
students with
Communication disorders, teaching
students with, **10**:17–30
interpersonal problems, **10**:27–30
language problems, **10**:20–27
speech problems, **10**:18–20
tips for teachers, **10**:19 (tab)
trends/issues influencing,
**10**:31–33
Communication skills, **3**:42
Communication/motility. *See*
Instructional adaptations, to
increase
Community collaboration,
**5**:7, **5**:43–46, **5**:55, **13**:48
Compensatory education,
**3**:10, **3**:77
Competitive employment,
**5**:24–25, **5**:55
Computer-assisted
instruction, **4**:5
Concentration game, **12**:41 (fig)
Concussion, **8**:25–26, **8**:63
Conductive hearing loss,
**7**:19, **7**:59

Conlon, C. J., **8**:14
Consultative (indirect) services,
**1**:26, **1**:40, **1**:41, **5**:12, **5**:55
Contextual variables, **4**:10, **4**:63
Continued education, **5**:26–27
Contusions, **8**:26, **8**:63
Convergent thinking,
**13**:17–18, **13**:52
Cooperative learning,
**4**:45–46, **4**:63
Corn, A., **7**:15
Corrective/supportive feedback,
**4**:40, **4**:46–47, **12**:37, **12**:43
Council for Children With
Behavioral Disorders, **11**:36
Council for Exceptional Children
(CEC), **12**:66
Counseling therapy,
**4**:43–45, **4**:63
*Covarrubias v. San Diego Unified
School District*, **2**:38 (tab)
Craniofacial anomalies,
**8**:22, **8**:63
Creative ability, **1**:34, **1**:40–41
Creative-productive giftedness,
**13**:43, **13**:52
Creech, B., **7**:26, **7**:42
Crisis therapy, **4**:44–45, **4**:63
Criterion-referenced tests, **3**:28–29,
**3**:77–78, **4**:9, **4**:64
Critical thinking, **4**:43
Crittenden, J. B., **7**:87
Crocker, A. C., **8**:13
Cued speech, **7**:39 (tab),
**7**:40–41, **7**:42
Cues
auditory, **7**:16, **7**:28, **7**:43
defining, **9**:56
phonetic, **9**:29, **9**:57
to improve math, **9**:32
to improve work
habits, **9**:36
to reduce behavior problems,
**10**:37, **11**:24
Curriculum compacting,
**13**:39, **13**:40
Curriculum-based assessment,
**3**:19–21, **3**:78, **9**:19

Curriculum-based measurement,
   **3**:21–22, **3**:78
Curriculum-referenced tests. *See*
   Criterion-referenced tests
Currie, J., **5**:15
Cystic fibrosis, **8**:12, **8**:63

D'Allura, T., **7**:14
D'Amico, R., **5**:24
Data collection, for assessments,
   **3**:25–31
Davidson, J. E., **13**:43
Davis, L., **12**:67
Deaf
   defining, **7**:18, **7**:21, **7**:59
   *See also* Deaf-and-blind/
      deaf-blind; Hearing
      impairments
Deaf culture, **7**:26, **7**:59
Deaf-and-blind/deaf-blind
   characteristics of, **7**:31–32
   defining, **7**:29–30, **7**:59–60
   prevalence of, **7**:30
Deafness and blindness,
   **1**:16, **1**:41, **7**:6, **7**:60
Deafness or hearing impairment,
   **1**:16, **1**:41
Deinstitutionalization,
   **5**:30, **5**:55
Delquadri, J., **4**:46
Dennis, R., **12**:59
Deno, S. L., **3**:22
Denton, P., **4**:45
Deshler, D., **4**:45
Developmental learning
   disabilities, **9**:51
Diabetes, **8**:11 (tab), **8**:63
Diagnostic tests, **3**:28, **3**:78
*Diana v. State Board of
   Education,* **2**:37 (tab)
Direct instruction,
   principles of, **4**:64
   corrective/supportive feedback,
      **4**:40, **4**:46–47, **12**:37, **12**:43
   independent practice,
      **4**:40, **10**:36–37
   modeling expected
      behavior, **4**:40

task analysis, **3**:22, **3**:81,
   **4**:10, **4**:40, **4**:65,
   **12**:43–45, **12**:72
*See also* Instruction
Direct services, **1**:25, **1**:41, **5**:12, **5**:55
Discrepancy
   defining, **9**:56
   dual, **9**:17–18
   eliminating, **9**:9
Discrepant scores, **3**:34, **3**:78, **12**:30
Discrimination, protection
   against, **1**:13
Distractibility (nonattention),
   **3**:47, **11**:47
Disturbed peer relations, **3**:47
Divergent thinking, **13**:17, **13**:52
Diverse students, **1**:29–31
Doorlag, D. H., **10**:18–20
Down syndrome, **12**:13–14,
   **12**:66, **12**:71
Drop out rate, **1**:30–31
Drug addiction, pregnancy
   and, **5**:10, **8**:14–15
DSM-IV, **9**:45 (tab)
Dual discrepancy, **9**:17–18
Due process, **1**:13, **1**:41, **2**:21,
   **2**:54, **2**:55
Duhaime, A., **8**:25, **8**:26, **8**:27
Dunn, Leota M., **10**:27
Dunn, Lloyd M., **10**:27
Duration recording, **3**:46, **3**:78

Early intervention
   as part of lifelong
      learning, **5**:50
   defining, **2**:55, **5**:55, **6**:44
   direct/indirect services for, **5**:12
   effectiveness of, **5**:14–16
   federal laws/incentives
      for, **5**:11–12
   for infants/toddlers, **2**:24
   Head Start, **5**:15
   home-based programs, **5**:12–13
   hospital-/center-based programs,
      **5**:13–14
   need for more programs, **5**:10
   preschool, **5**:9–10
   social factor influence on, **6**:9–10

special education services,
   **5**:10–11 (fig)
Ypsilanti Perry Preschool
   Project, **5**:15–16
E-books, **9**:29
Echolalia, **8**:41, **11**:14
Ecobehavioral assessment,
   **3**:22–23, **3**:78
Edelman, S., **12**:59
Education, defining, **1**:9, **1**:41
Education for All Handicapped
   Children Act, **1**:12;
   **2**:11 (tab), **1**:19
   amendments to, **2**:24–25, **2**:48–49
   defining, **2**:56
   early childhood education and,
      **5**:11–12
   objectives of, **2**:15
   problems addressed by, **2**:15–16
   provisions of
      (*See* Individualized
      education programs; Least
      restrictive environment;
      Protection in evaluation
      procedures)
   specific learning disabilities and,
      **9**:11–12
   specific procedures of, **2**:16
   *See also* Individuals With
      Disabilities Education Act
Educational settings
   diverse, **1**:31–32
   variations by state, **1**:32
   *See also* Least restrictive
      environment
Egel, A. L., **8**:30
Ekwall, E., **3**:38
Electronic travel aids, **4**:55–56, **4**:64
Elementary and Secondary
   Education Act (ESEA). *See*
   No Child Left Behind Act
Eligibility decisions, **1**:22, **3**:14–15,
   **3**:78, **7**:9–10, **7**:55
Elliott, J., **4**:5
Emotional disturbance
   academic characteristics of,
      **11**:10–11
   anxiety, **11**:18–22

behavior intervention plans,
   **11**:15–16
behavioral characteristics of,
   **11**:12–14
cognitive characteristics of,
   **11**:9–10
communication characteristics
   of, **11**:14
defining, **1**:16, **1**:41, **11**:7–9,
   **11**:35–37, **11**:39–40
functional behavioral assessment
   and, **11**:15–16
improving social interactions,
   **11**:13–14
medical treatment for, **11**:37–38
physical characteristics of,
   **11**:11–12
psychosomatic, **11**:11
terms used to describe,
   **11**:10 (tab)
*See also* Emotional disturbance,
   teaching students with
Emotional disturbance, teaching
   students with
   anxiety, **11**:18–22
   behavior intervention plans,
      **11**:17–26
   disruptiveness, **11**:27–29
   nonattention (distractibility),
      **11**:29–30
   school opposition/
      noncompliance, **11**:23 (tab)
   social problems, **11**:27–33
   task avoidance, **11**:31–33
   temper tantrums, **11**:24–26
   tips for school opposition/
      noncompliance, **11**:23 (tab)
   tips for school phobia, **11**:21 (tips)
   tips for teachers of, **11**:18 (tab)
   tips for temper tantrums,
      **11**:25–26
   tips for test-taking, **11**:22 (tab)
   trends/issues influencing,
      **11**:35–37
Emotional problems, **11**:17, **11**:47
Employment, sheltered/ supported,
   **5**:25, **5**:56
Empowerment movement, **7**:47

Enhanced image devices,
    **7:**36–37, **7:**60
Enrichment, **3:**10, **3:**78,
    **13:**23–24, **13:**28–36, **13:**53
Enright, B., **3:**21
Entwistle, D., **4:**5
Entwistle, N., **4:**5
Epidural hematomas, **8:**26, **8:**64
Epilepsy, **8:**23, **8:**64
Epilepsy Foundation
    of America, **8:**47
Epstein, A., **5:**16
Epstein, J. L.
Equal access, **2:**14, **2:**41 (tab), 45–46
Equal protection clause,
    **2:**7–8, **2:**53, **2:**55
ERIC Clearinghouse on Disabilities
    and Gifted Education, **1:**11
Erin, J. N., **7:**8
Error analysis, **3:**38, **3:**78
Errors
    assessment, **3:**62–63
    halo effect, **3:**62
    integration, **3:**48
    logical, **3:**62
    of central tendency, **3:**62
    of leniency, **3:**62
    perseveration, **3:**38, **3:**48
    rotation, **3:**48
    sensitivity, **3:**62
Errors of central tendency, **3:**62
Errors of leniency, **3:**62
Ethell, R. G., **4:**5
Evaluation
    defining, **4:**64
    formative, **4:**23, **4:**64
    language, **10:**44
    process, **1:**24
    program, **3:**16–17, **3:**80
    progress, **1:**24, **3:**80
    protection in procedures,
        **1:**13, **1:**42, **2:**21–23, **2:**56
    speech, **10:**44
    summative, **4:**23, **4:**65
Event recording, **3:**46, **3:**78
Exceptional students, defining, **1:**41
Exceptionality decisions,
    **3:**12, **3:**78–79

Exclusion, **2:**19 (fig),
    **2:**42 (tab), **2:**49–50
Expressive language, **10:**43

Face validity, **3:**57, **3:**79
Families/community agencies. *See*
    Community collaboration;
    Early intervention; Family
    involvement; Transition
    services
Family involvement, **5:**7
    adverse affects of disability on
        family, **5:**38
    affect of exceptionalities on
        families, **5:**35–37
    gifted student concerns, **5:**37–38
    home–school
        collaboration barriers, **5:**41
        (tab)–42 (tab)
    home–school collaboration
        barriers, overcoming,
        **5:**39–40, **5:**42
    institutionalization *vs.* home care
        issues, **5:**38
    types of, **5:**39
    with communication disorders,
        **10:**30
FAPE (free and appropriate
    education), **2:**55
Fazzi, D. L., **7:**7, **7:**11
Feedback
    auditory, **7:**37
    corrective/supportive, **4:**46–47,
        **12:**37, **12:**43
    defining, **4:**21, **4:**64
    tactile, **7:**31
Fetal alcohol syndrome,
    **5:**10, **8:**14, **8:**64
Finger spelling, **7:**40, **7:**60
Flexible promotion, **13:**25
Flexible scheduling,
    **3:**71, **4:**54, **4:**64
Flexible settings, **3:**71, **4:**54, **4:**64
Fluency disorder, **10:**10, **10:**43
Forlenza-Bailey, A., **4:**5
Formal assessments, **3:**11
Formal interviews, **3:**30
Formal observations, **3:**27, **3:**29

Formal tests, **3:**27, **3:**79
Formative evaluation, **4:**23, **4:**64
Forster, G., **6:**53
Foster, R., **10:**27
Foster homes, **5:**31–32
*Frederick L. v. Thomas,*
    **2:**39 (tab)–40 (tab)
Free and appropriate education
    (FAPE), **2:**55
Frequency, **7:**20 (tab), **7:**60
Fristoe, M., **10:**26
Fuchs, D., **9:**17
Full inclusion, **6:**21
Functional academic assessment,
    **9:**19, **9:**57
Functional behavioral assessment,
    **9:**19, **9:**57, **11:**15–16, **11:**47
Functional hearing losses, **7:**24, **7:**25
    (tab), **7:**60
Funding, **6:**15, **6:**16–17, **6:**44

Gallagher, J., **13:**11,
    **13:**19, **13:**20, **13:**45
Gallaudet Research Institute
    (GRI), **7:**22
Gallup, A. M., **11:**39
Gardner, H., **13:**43
Giangreco, M. F., **12:**59
Gickling, E., **3:**20
Giddan, J. J., **10:**27
Gifted, defining, **13:**53
Gifted and Talented Children's
    Education Act, **1:**33–34,
    **13:**10–11
Gifted and talented students
    academic characteristics of,
        **13:**18–19
    behavioral characteristics of,
        **13:**20–21
    characteristics of,
        **13:**15–22, **13:**16 (tab)–17 (tab)
    cognitive characteristics of,
        **13:**15–18
    communication characteristics of,
        **13:**21–22
    concerns of families with,
        **5:**37–38
    creative ability, **1:**34, **1:**40

creative-productive giftedness,
    **13:**43
criteria other than intelligence
    test to determine, **13:**42–43
defining, **1:**16, **1:**41
evolving concept of giftedness,
    **13:**41–42
federal legislation concerning,
    **13:**9–11
identifying gifts/talents, **1:**35–36
identifying students as, **13:**12–14
intellectual ability of, **1:**34
leadership ability of, **1:**35
physical characteristics of,
    **13:**19–20
schoolhouse
    giftedness, **13:**43
specific academic ability, **1:**34–35
state definitions of, **13:**11–12
terms used to describe,
    **13:**10 (tab)
underrepresented groups in
    category of, **13:**44–45
visual/performing arts ability of,
    **1:**35, **1:**40
*See also* Gifted and talented
    students, teaching
Gifted and talented students,
    teaching
    acceleration tactics, **13:**36–40
    acceleration/advancement
        approach, **13:**25–27
    criteria other than intelligence
        test, **13:**42–43
    enrichment approach, **13:**23–24
    enrichment tactics, **13:**28–36
    extending knowledge in content
        areas, **13:**31–33
    extending knowledge into new
        areas, **13:**33–36 (fig)
    practicing/polishing skills,
        **13:**28–31 (fig)
    teacher tips, **13:**24 (tab), **13:**45–46
    trends/issues influencing,
        **13:**41–46
Glaser, W., **4:**43
Goals 2000: The Educate America
    Act, **6:**31, **6:**33

adult literacy/lifelong learning,
6:27–28
advocacy, 6:12–13
applying to child with special
needs, 6:30
mathematics/science, 6:27
overview of, 6:22,
6:23 (tab)–6:24 (tab)
parental participation, 6:29
safe/disciplined and
alcohol-/drug-free
schools, 6:28–29
school completion, 6:24–25
school readiness, 6:22, 6:24
standards, 6:31, 6:33
student achievement/
citizenship, 6:25–26
teacher education/ professional
development, 6:26–27
See also Individuals With
Disabilities Education Act;
No Child Left Behind Act
Goldman, R., 10:26
Good, T., 4:13
Goss v. Lopez, 2:39 (tab)
Grammar, 10:44
Grand mal (tonic-clonic) seizures,
8:23, 8:64
Gray Oral Reading Test–4, 3:37
Greene, J. P., 6:53
Greenwood, C., 3:22, 4:46
Greer, B. B., 8:49
Greer, J. G., 8:49
GRI (Gallaudet Research
Institute), 7:22
Griffin, N. S., 13:11
Grossman, H., 12:24–25
Group data, 3:50
Group homes, 5:30–31, 5:55
Group-administered
tests, 3:27, 3:79
Gruenewald, L., 12:67
Guertin, T. L., 13:45
Guide dogs, 4:55

Hairston v. Drosick, 2:39 (tab)
Hall, V., 4:46
Halo effect errors, 3:62

Haloed, 3:56
Handicapped Children's
Early Education
Assistance Act, 5:11
Handicapped Children's Protection
Act, 2:48–49, 2:55
Harcourt Educational
Measurement, 3:37
Hard-of-hearing
defining, 7:18–19, 7:21, 7:60
See also Hearing impairments
Hart, C. A., 8:30
Haskins, R., 5:15
Havertape, J., 3:20
Head Start, 5:11, 5:15,
5:55, 6:7, 6:9
HeadSmart Schools program,
8:27–28
Hearing acuity, 3:40
Hearing aid, 4:50–51, 4:64, 7:41
troubleshooting, 7:50–51
Hearing impairments
academic characteristics of,
7:23–24
behavioral characteristics of,
7:24–27
central hearing losses, 7:57
cognitive characteristics of,
7:22–23
communication characteristics of,
7:27–28 (tab)
conductive hearing losses,
7:19, 7:56
deaf culture and, 7:26, 7:59
defining, 7:6, 7:18, 7:60
educational implications of,
7:57–58
ethnicity and, 7:26
functional hearing losses, 7:24,
7:25 (tab), 7:60
history of schools for deaf
students, 7:17–18
integrating deaf/hearing
students, 7:26–27
manual communication
for, 7:58
measuring hearing loss, 7:19–21
mixed hearing losses, 7:57

oral communication for, **7:**58
prevalence of, **7:**21–22, **7:**56
senorineural losses, **7:**19, **7:**56–57
signs of, **7:**28 (tab)
teacher tips, **7:**28 (tab)
technology for, **7:**58
total communication for, **7:**58
*See also* Deaf-and-blind/
deaf-blind
Heart conditions, **8:**12, **8:**64
Hebbeler, K., **5:**24
Hematomas, **8:**26, **8:**64
subdural, **8:**26, **8:**66
Hemophilia, **8:**13, **8:**59, **8:**64
Henderson, A. T., **5:**42 (tab)
*Hendrick Hudson District Board
of Education v. Rowley,*
**2:**41 (tab), **2:**45–46
Highly qualified teacher, **2:**31–32
Ho, A. S. P., **4:**5
*Hobson v. Hansen,* **2:**36 (tab)
Hodgkinson, H. L., 44
Holmes, D. L., **8:**29
Home-based programs,
**5:**12–14, **5:**55
Homeless child/wards of
court, **2:**34
Homework buddies, **9:**38–39
*Honig v. Doe,* **2:**19 (fig), **2:**42 (tab),
**2:**49–50
Hospital-based programs, **5:**13–14,
**5:**55
Humphries, T., **7:**26
Hunsaker, S. L., **1:**35–36
Hyperactivity-impulsivity, **9:**23–24,
**9:**45 (tab), **9:**57
Hyperopia, **7:**9–10, **7:**60

IDEA. *See* Individuals With
Disabilities Education Act
IDEIA. *See* Individuals With
Disabilities Education
Improvement Act
IEP. *See* Individualized education
programs
IFSP (individualized family service
plan), **2:**25, **2:**54, **2:**55, **12:**71
Imber-Black, E., **5:**42 (tab)

Immaturity, **3:**47
Immunodeficiency, **8:**12
Inattention, **9:**46–47, **9:**57
Incidental learning, **7:**14
In-class field trip, for math skills,
**12:**42 (fig)
Inclusion, **1:**21–22, **1:**41, **6:**21, **6:**38–39
as school reform, **6:**21, **6:**38–39
defining, **6:**45
full, **6:**21
mainstreaming as, **2:**54, **2:**56,
**5:**29–30, **5:**56
of student with medical/
physical/multiple
disabilities, **8:**56–59,
**8:**57 (tab)
of student with mental
retardation, **12:**67–68
technology role in, **6:**38–39
*See also* Least restrictive
environment
Independent living,
**5:**23, **5:**30, **5:**32, **8:**31,
**12:**31, **12:**55, **12:**58
Independent practice, **4:**40, **10:**36–37
Indirect (consultative)
services, **1:**26, **1:**40,
**1:**41, **5:**12, **5:**55
Individual data, **3:**50
Individual family service plan
(IFSP), **5:**12, **5:**55, **12:**33
Individualized education programs
(IEP), **1:**13, **1:**23–24, **2:**54, **8:**43
amendments to, **2:**33
decision-making process
and, **2:**23–2:**24
defining, **1:**42, **2:**55, **3:**79
due process hearing, **2:**21
for student with communication
disorder, **10:**41–42
for student with mental
retardation, **12:**6–7,
**12:**33, **12:**71
individualized family
service plan, **2:**25,
**2:**54, **2:**55, **12:**71
least restrictive environment
requirement of, **2:**23

measurable goals requirement of,
2:17, 2:28
prior written notice requirement
of, 2:21
protection in evaluation
procedures provision
of, 2:21
reasons for, 2:17, 2:20
sample of, 2:18 (fig)–19 (fig)
team members required by,
2:20 (fig)
Individualized family service plan
(IFSP), 2:25, 2:54, 2:55, 12:71
Individualized transition plan (ITP),
2:26, 2:55–56, 5:23,
5:56, 12:63, 12:71
Individually administered tests, 3:27
Individuals With Disabilities
Education Act (IDEA),
2:12 (tab), 2:25–26, 2:54
assistive technologies under, 2:26
defining, 2:56
discrimination protection, 1:13
mandates of, 1:12–13,
4:54, 6:37–38
on educational settings, 1:31–32
on emotional disturbance, 11:7–8,
11:35–36
on learning disabilities, 9:7–8, 9:9
on mental retardation, 12:9
on transition services, 5:23
preschool services under,
5:10–11 (fig)
See also Education for All
Handicapped Children Act;
Individuals With Disabilities
Education Act (IDEA),
amendments to; Individuals
With Disabilities Education
Improvement Act; Least
restrictive environment
Individuals With Disabilities
Education Act (IDEA),
amendments to
discipline policies, 2:28–29
individualized education
program, 2:28
manifestation determination, 2:29

parental consent for reevaluation,
2:12 (tab), 2:27
preschoolers, 5:12
streamlined reevaluation, 2:27–28
Individuals With Disabilities
Education Improvement Act
(IDEIA), 2:13, 2:25–26, 2:56
assessment language/
communication mode,
2:32–33
highly qualified teacher
requirement, 2:31–32
homeless child/wards
of court, 2:34
individualized education
program provisions, 2:33
learning disabled
identification, 2:32
special education students in
general education, 2:33
transition planning, 2:33
Inference, 3:61–62, 3:79
Informal interviews, 3:30, 3:79
Informal observations,
3:27, 3:29, 3:44
Informal tests, 3:27, 3:79
Institutions, for adults with
special needs, 5:33
Instruction
computer-assisted, 4:5
defining, 4:5, 4:7, 4:64
teaching as, 4:5
See also Direct instruction,
principles of; Instruction,
adapting for students with
special needs; Instruction,
delivering; Instruction,
evaluating; Instruction,
managing; Instruction,
planning
Instruction, adapting for students
with special
needs, 4:31–38
ability training, 4:39–40
behavior therapy, 4:38
classwide peer tutoring, 4:47
cognitive behavior modification,
4:41, 4:42 (fig)

cognitive skills training, **4:**41, **4:**43
cooperative learning, **4:**45–46
counseling therapy, **4:**43–45
critical thinking, **4:**43
direct instruction, **4:**40
learning strategies training, **4:**45
peer tutoring, **4:**46
peer-directed learning, **4:**46
precision teaching, **4:**39
social skills training, **4:**47–48
Instruction, delivering, **4:**17–23
adjusting instruction, **4:**21 (tab),
      **4:**22–23
monitoring student learning,
      **4:**21 (tab)–22
motivating students, **4:**20
overview of, **4:**18 (tab)
presenting content, **4:**17–20
presenting lessons, **4:**17–19
providing relevant
      practice, **4:**20
teaching thinking skills, **4:**19–20
Instruction, evaluating, **4:**23–29
informing students of
      progress, **4:**27
maintaining student progress
      records, **4:**26 (fig)–27
making judgments about student
      performance, **4:**28 (fig)–29
monitoring engaged time, **4:**25
monitoring student
      understanding, **4:**23–25
overview of, **4:**24 (tab)
using data to make decisions,
      **4:**27–28
Instruction, managing, **4:**14–17
creating positive environment,
      **4:**16–17
overview of, **4:**15 (tab)
preparing for instruction,
      **4:**15–16
using time productively, **4:**16
Instruction, planning, **4:**7–14
actively involving
      students, **4:**14
analyzing groupings, **4:**10–11
analyzing task, **4:**10
assessing student skills, **4:**9

communicating realistic
      expectations, **4:**13–14
considering contextual
      variables, **4:**10
deciding how to teach, **4:**11–13
deciding what to teach, **4:**9–11
establishing gaps in actual/
      expected performance, **4:**11
establishing sequence, **4:**10
explicitly stating
      expectations, **4:**14
maintaining high
      standards, **4:**14
monitoring
      performance/replanning
      instruction, **4:**13
overview of, **4:**8 (tab)
pacing, **4:**13
selecting methods/materials,
      **4:**12–13
setting goals, **4:**12
Instructional adaptations, to
      increase communication/
      motility, **4:**49–50
amplification systems, **4:**51
braille, **4:**52, **7:**10, **7:**13,
      **7:**15, **7:**16, **7:**34, **7:**35 (tab)
calculators, **4:**53
canes, **4:**55
communication
      boards, **4:**50
computers, **4:**53–54
electronic travel aids, **4:**55–56
guide dogs, **4:**55
hearing aids, **4:**50–51
Kurzweil reading
      machines, **4:**53
optacons, **4:**52–53
prostheses, **4:**56–57
telecommunication devices,
      **4:**51–52
test modifications, **4:**54
wheelchairs, **4:**56
Instructional diagnosis, **3:**22, **3:**79
Instructional programs, keys
      to success in, **5:**47–50
commitment to normal life
      experiences, **5:**49

commitment to remedial
    programming, **5**:49
compatible physical
    environment, **5**:49
encouraging appropriate
    behavior, **5**:50
individualized planning, **5**:48–49
lifelong learning, **5**:50
Integration errors, **3**:48
Intellectual abilities, **1**:34, **1**:42, **2**:32,
    **3**:34–37, **9**:9
    intelligence interviews, **3**:36–37
    observing intelligence, **3**:34, 36
    overview of, **3**:35 (tab)–36 (tab)
    testing intelligence, **3**:34
Intellectual functioning, **12**:71
Intelligence. *See* Intellectual abilities
International Baccalaureate
    (IB), **13**:26
Interval recording, **3**:45, **3**:79
Intervention assistance. *See*
    Prereferral interventions
Intervention assistance team (IAT),
    **3**:10, **3**:79
Interviews, **3**:26, **3**:30–31
    academic achievement,
        assessing, **3**:38–39
    formal, **3**:30
    informal, **3**:30, **3**:79
    intelligence, **3**:36–37
    language, **3**:44
    perceptual-motor, **3**:48
    psychological, **3**:46–47
    structured, **3**:30
    to assess academic achievement,
        **3**:38–39
    unstructured, **3**:30
Irrelevant activity, **11**:31, **11**:47
*Irving Independent School District v.
    Tatro*, **2**:42 (tab), **2**:46, **2**:54
ITP (individualized transition plan),
    **2**:26, **2**:55–56, **5**:23, **5**:56,
    **12**:63, **12**:71

Jackson, D. W., **7**:23, **7**:24,
    **7**:27, **7**:40, **7**:42
Jakob K. Javits Gifted and Talented
    Students Act, **13**:11

Jatho, J., **7**:26, **7**:42
Job coach, **5**:25, **5**:48, **5**:56, **12**:54
Johnson, D. W., **4**:45
Johnson, F., **12**:67
Johnson, N. E., **13**:45
Johnson, R. T., **4**:45
Jorgensen, J., **12**:67
Journals/articles (resources)
    assessment, **3**:92–93
    communication disorders,
        **10**:57–58
    emotional disturbance, **11**:60–63
    fundamentals of special
        education, **1**:54–55
    gifted and talented child, **13**:64
    learning disabilities, **9**:67–68
    legal foundations, **2**:66
    medical/physical/multiple
        disabilities, **8**:80–82
    mental retardation, **12**:84–85
    public policy/school
        reform, **6**:56
    sensory disabilities, **7**:77–79
    transitions, **5**:67
Juvenile rheumatoid arthritis,
    **8**:20, **8**:64

Kanner, Leo, **8**:29
Kember, D., **4**:5
Kentucky School System
    reform, **6**:34–35
*Kevin T. v. Elmhurst Community
    School District No.*, **2**:44 (tab)
Key Points
    assessment, **3**:75–76
    communication disorders,
        **10**:42–43
    effective instruction, **4**:61–62
    emotional disturbance, **11**:43–46
    fundamentals, **1**:39–40
    gifted and talented child,
        **13**:51–52
    learning disabilities, **9**:55–56
    legal foundations, **2**:53–54
    medical/physical/multiple
        disabilities, **8**:61–62
    mental retardation,
        **12**:69–70

public policy/school reform,
6:43–44
sensory disabilities, 7:53–58
transitions, 5:53–54
Key Vocabulary
assessment, 3:76–81
communication disorders,
10:43–45
effective instruction, 4:62–66
emotional disturbance, 11:46–47
families/community agencies,
5:54–56
fundamentals, 1:40–43
gifted and talented child,
13:52–53
learning disabilities, 9:56–57
legal foundations, 2:54–56
medical/physical/multiple
disabilities, 8:62–66
mental retardation, 12:70–72
public policy/school reform,
6:44–46
sensory disabilities, 7:59–62
Kirk, S. A., 9:51
Klinefelter syndrome, 12:14, 12:71
Koestler, F., 7:8
Koppitz, E. M., 3:47
Kreimeyer, K. H., 7:26
Kurzweil reading machines, 4:53
Kwan, K. P., 4:5

Lagomarcino, T., 5:24
Lahey, B. B., 9:44
Language development, 3:43–44
language test components, 3:43
using interviews, 3:44
using observations, 3:44
Language disorders, 10:44
Language evaluation, 10:44
*Larry P v. Riles,* 2:38 (tab)–39 (tab),
6:10, 6:45
Larsen, L. M., 13:11
Larsen, M. D., 13:11
Latency recording, 3:46, 3:80
Law, continuing changes in, 2:7
Lead poisoning, 8:11 (tab), 8:64
Leadership ability, 1:35, 1:42,
13:10, 13:42

Learning centers,
for reading, 9:31
Learning disabilities (LDs)
academic, 9:51
academic characteristics
of, 9:23
assessing, 9:17–19
behavioral characteristics of,
9:23–24
category growth, 9:12, 9:14
causes of, 9:15–16
cognitive characteristics of, 9:22
communication characteristics of,
9:24–25
criteria for identifying, 9:8–9
defining, 9:7–8, 9:49–50, 9:57
defining, variations by state,
9:51–52
developmental, 9:51
discrepancy criterion
removal, 9:9
distribution of students
with, by state, 9:13
(tab)–9:14 (tab)
growth in specific learning
disabilities category, 9:11–12
physical characteristics
of, 9:23
prevalence of, 9:11
subtypes of, 9:51
transition of students
with, 9:52
*See also* Learning disabilities
(LDs), improving classroom
behavior for students with;
Learning disabilities (LDs),
teaching students with
Learning disabilities (LDs),
improving classroom behavior
for students with
daily reports, 9:37 (fig)
homework buddies,
9:38–39
study skills, 9:37–39
work habits, 9:35–37
Learning disabilities (LDs),
teaching students with,
9:25–41

general interventions, **9:**26 (tab)
math skills, **9:**32–33
reading skills, **9:**27–32
social relations, **9:**39–41
study skills, **9:**37–39
trends/issues influencing
teaching of, **9:**49–52
work habits, **9:**35–37
written language skills, **9:**33–35
Learning strategies training,
**4:**45, **4:**64
Least restrictive environment (LRE),
**1:**13, **1:**27–28, **2:**23, **2:**41, **2:**54,
**2:**56, **12:**61
defining, **5:**30, **5:**56, **12:**71
Ledesma, J., **4:**5
Lee, V. E., **5:**15
Leff, D., **7:**11, **7:**15
Legal fees, **2:**42 (tab), **2:**46–48
Legal foundations, of special
education
balance perspective in, **2:**51–52
brief history of, **2:**9–10
early issues in, **2:**44–45
overview of important laws,
**2:**10–11
overview of influential court
cases, **2:**36 (tab)–44 (tab)
Supreme Court rulings, **2:**45–50
See also *individual laws and
individual cases*
Legally blind, **7:**9, **7:**60
Legg-Calvé-Perthes disease,
**8:**21, **8:**64
Lehr, C., **5:**18
Lehr, F., **9:**28
*Lemon v. Bossier Parish School Board,*
**2:**38 (tab)
Leukemia, **8:**11 (tab), **8:**64
Leventhal, J. D., **7:**36
Levine, D. U., **4:**5–6
Levy, S. E., **8:**15
Lewis, R. B., **8:**56–58, **8:**57 (tab),
**10:**18–20
Lieberman, L., **7:**29
Lifelong learning, **5:**50, **6:**27–28
*Light v. Parkway School District,*
**2:**43 (tab)

Liles, C., **8:**15–16, **8:**43, **8:**55–56
Limb deficiencies, **8:**21–22, **8:**64
Listening-skills training,
**7:**34, **7:**35 (tab)
Living arrangements, for adults
with special needs
alternative living unit, **5:**31
foster homes, **5:**31–32
group homes, **5:**30–31
independent living, **5:**32
institutions, **5:**33
Lloyd, J., **4:**40
Logical errors, **3:**62
Long, E., **12:**67
*Lora v. New York City Board of
Education,* **2:**40 (tab)–41 (tab)
Loudness, **7:**19–20, **7:**60
Louisiana Department of Education,
**13:**12
Low vision, **7:**60–61
Luckner, J., **7:**24, **7:**38, **7:**42, **7:**50
Luetke-Stahlman, B., **7:**24, **7:**42, **7:**50
Lynch, E. W., **8:**56–58, **8:**57 (tab)

Mainstreaming, **2:**54, **2:**56,
**5:**29–30, **5:**56
*See also* Least restrictive
environment
Mangrum, C. II, **5:**26
Manifestation determination,
**2:**29, **2:**56
Manual movements, **7:**40, **7:**61
Marburger, C. L., **5:**42 (tab)
Marder, C., **5:**24
Marland, S., **13:**41–42
Maryland State Department of
Education, **13:**11
Mastery, defining, **9:**32
Mathematics, improving,
**6:**27, **9:**32–33, **9:**34 (fig)
McBurnett, K., **9:**44
McKinney, J. D., **9:**51
McMeniman, M. M., **4:**5
Measures of process disorders,
**9:**18–19
Medical disabilities, **8:**9–16
AIDS, **8:**12–13
cystic fibrosis, **8:**12

fetal alcohol syndrome, **8**:14
heart conditions, **8**:12
hemophilia, **8**:13–14
identification by medical
    symptoms, **8**:9–10
maternal cocaine use, **8**:14–15
medically fragile/technology
    dependent groups, **8**:15–16
other health impairments,
    **8**:10–11 (tab)
prevalence of, **8**:10
special health problems, **8**:14–15
Medical procedures, to ensure
    appropriate education,
    **2**:46, **2**:48, **2**:54
Medical treatment, for emotional
    disturbance, **11**:37–38
Medically fragile, **8**:15, **8**:64
Medical/physical/multiple
    disabilities
    academic characteristics
        of, **8**:38
    behavioral characteristics of,
        **8**:39–40
    cognitive characteristics of,
        **8**:37–38
    communication characteristics of,
        **8**:40–41
    distribution of child with, **8**:7–8
        (fig)
    home *vs.* institutional care for,
        **8**:55–56
    inclusion of student with, **8**:56
    inclusion of student with,
        overcoming barriers to,
        **8**:56–59, **8**:57 (tab)
    medical disabilities, **8**:9–16,
        **8**:10–11 (tab)
    multiple disabilities, **8**:33–35
    physical characteristics of, **8**:39
    physical disabilities,
        **8**:17–31, **8**:25 (tab)
    relationship to federal disability
        categories, **8**:7 (fig)
    *See also* Medical/
        physical/multiple
        disabilities, teaching
        students with

Medical/physical/multiple
    disabilities, teaching students
    with, **8**:43–53
    adapting instruction, **8**:47–49
    common adaptations, **8**:49–50
    encouraging socialization, **8**:53
    facilitating communication,
        **8**:50–52
    fostering independence, **8**:52–53
    general tips for, **8**:45 (tab)
    identifying disabilities, **8**:44
    key areas of assistance, **8**:46–47
    questions to ask about, **8**:44, **8**:45
        (tab)–**8**:46 (tab)
    residual functioning, **8**:52–53
Mental retardation, **1**:16, **1**:42
    academic characteristics of, **12**:30
    as primary/secondary condition,
        **12**:28
    behavioral characteristics
        of, **12**:31
    characteristics of, **12**:2 (tab)
    cognitive characteristics
        of, **12**:30
    communication characteristics of,
        **12**:31–32
    defining, **12**:6, **12**:9, **12**:71
    genetic conditions as cause
        of, **12**:13–14
    graduation rates of student with,
        **12**:63–64
    health problems as cause
        of, **12**:15
    inclusion of student with,
        **12**:67–68
    individualized education
        program, **12**:6–7
    learning environments for
        student with, **12**:67
    mild/moderate/severe/
        profound retardation, **12**:10
        (fig)–**12**:11 (tab)
    physical characteristics of,
        **12**:30–31
    prevalence of, **12**:11
    preventing, **12**:62 (tab)
    problems during pregnancy/
        birth as cause of, **12**:15

recent advances in treatment/
    services, **12:**65–67
self-determination
    and, **12:**64
transitioning from school to
    work, **12:**63–64
*See also* Mental retardation,
    diagnosing; Mental
    retardation, teaching
    students with
Mental retardation, diagnosing,
    **12:**17–25
  adaptive behavior area,
    **12:**17, **12:**19–25
  adaptive behavior, defining,
    **12:**21
  adaptive behavior scales, **12:**21
  adaptive skill areas evaluated,
    **12:**21 (tab)–23 (tab)
  age-related criteria for, **12:**24–25
  intellectual functioning
    area, **12:**17
Mental retardation, teaching
    students with, **12:**33–51
  by making adaptations, **12:**33–34
  family tips for, **12:**34,
    **12:**36 (tab)
  functional math skills,
    **12:**41–42 (fig)
  functional reading skills, **12:**38–41
    (fig), **12:**39 (fig), **12:**40
    (fig), **12:**41 (fig), 40 (fig)
  functional writing, **12:**40
  general interventions for,
    **12:**37 (tab)
  grading systems for, **12:**47–49
  individualized education
    program, **12:**33
  individualized family services
    plan, **12:**33
  leisure skills, **12:**50–51
  school adaptive behavior,
    **12:**45–49
  task analysis, **12:**43–45
  task completion, **12:**38
  teacher tips for, **12:**35 (tab)
  trends/issues influencing,
    **12:**61–64

work skills, **12:**49–50
    *See also* Severe disabilities,
        teaching student with
*Metropolitan Achievement Tests,* **3:**37
Meyer, C., **3:**39
Meyer, L. H., **12:**55
Michaud, L. J., **8:**25, **8:**26, **8:**27
Mild/moderate/severe/
    profound retardation,
    **12:**10 (fig)–**12:**11 (tab)
Miller, L., **3:**21
Minitests, **9:**30 (fig), **9:**57
*Minnesota Standards for
    Services to Gifted and
    Talented Students,* **13:**12
Minnesota State Advisory
    Council for the Gifted
    and Talented, **13:**12
Mizuko, M., **10:**16
Mobility, **7:**14, **7:**61
Mobility aids, **7:**34, **7:**35 (tab)
Mock, D., **9:**17
Molloy, D. E., **9:**17–18
Moore, S. D., **1:**35–36
Moores, D., **7:**17, **7:**21,
    **7:**23, **7:**24–25, **7:**26, **7:**42
Moran, M., **6:**41
Morgan, P. L., **9:**17
Morphology, **10:**10–11, **10:**44
Mowat Sensor, **4:**55–56
Muir, S., **7:**38
Multiple disabilities, **8:**34–35
Multiple intelligences, **13:**43, **13:**53
Multiple or severe
    disabilities, **1:**16, **1:**42
    *See also* Severe disabilities,
        teaching student with
Multiple sclerosis, **8:**20–21
Murphy, D. S., **8:**56–58, **8:**57 (tab)
Muscular dystrophy, **8:**19–20, **8:**65
Myelomeningocele, **8:**24
Myopia, **7:**9, **7:**61

NAGC (National Association for
    Gifted Children), **13:**25–27
Nania, P. A., **5:**18
*A Nation at Risk: The Imperative for
    Educational Reform,* **6:**19–20

National Association for
Gifted Children (NAGC),
**13**:25–27
National Association
of the Deaf, **7**:42
National Autistic Society, **8**:28
National Center for Education
Statistics, **1**:31, **5**:9, **5**:10
National Commission on Excellence
in Education, **6**:19–20
National Council on Educational
Standards and Testing, **6**:31–32
National Dissemination Center for
Children with Disabilities
(NICHY), **11**:44–46
National Education Goals,
**5**:10, **6**:19–20, **6**:45
National Educational
Standards and Improvement
Council, **6**:31
National Governors' Association,
**6**:20, **6**:34
National Head Injury Foundation
(NHIF), **8**:27–28
National Information Center, **10**:38
National Institute on Deafness and
Other Communication
Disorders Information
Clearinghouse, **7**:58
National Joint Committee on
Learning Disabilities (NJCLD),
**9**:15, **9**:50
National Research Council, **1**:13
Nechita, A., **1**:35
Needs assessments, **4**:41, **4**:64
Nephrosis/nephritis,
**8**:11 (tab), **8**:65
Neurological disorders, **8**:22–25
cerebral palsy, **8**:23–24
epilepsy, **8**:23
overview of, **8**:25 (tab)
spina bifida, **8**:24
spinal cord injury, **8**:24–25
Newland, T. E.,
**7**:12–13, **7**:30
Newman, L., **5**:24
NHIF (National Head Injury
Foundation), **8**:27–28

NICHY (National Dissemination
Center for Children with
Disabilities), **11**:44–46
NJCLD (National Joint Committee
on Learning Disabilities),
**9**:15, **9**:50
No Child Left Behind Act, **2**:12 (tab),
**2**:29–31, **2**:54, **6**:10, **6**:37–38, **6**:45
Nonattention (distractibility),
**11**:29–30, **11**:47
Noncategorical, **12**:18, **12**:71
Noncompliance (oppositional
behavior), **11**:22–24, **11**:47
Nonmanual movements, **7**:40, **7**:61
Nonphysical disruptions,
**11**:27–28, **11**:47
Normal field of vision, **7**:9, **7**:61
Normalization, **12**:61, **12**:72
Normative peer comparisons,
**4**:28, **4**:64
Norm-referenced tests,
**3**:29, **3**:80, **4**:9, **4**:64
Norms, **3**:8–9, **3**:80
Nystagmus, **7**:10, **7**:61

Objective-referenced test. *See*
Criterion-referenced tests
Observations, **3**:25–26, **3**:29–30
active, **3**:29, **3**:77
defining, **3**:80
formal, **3**:29
informal, **3**:27, **3**:29, **3**:44
language, **3**:44
of achievement, **3**:38
of sensory acuity, **3**:40–41
passive, **3**:29, **3**:80
perceptual-motor, **3**:48
Occupational and
social skills, **3**:42
OCR (Optical character recognition),
**7**:36 (tab),
**7**:38, **7**:61
Ocular motility, **7**:10, **7**:61
Oden, M., **13**:20, **13**:41, **13**:42
Office of Civil Rights, **6**:11, **6**:13
Office of Educational Research
and Improvement, **13**:45,
**13**:48, **13**:49

Office of Special
    Education Programs (OSEP),
    **6**:13–14, **6**:45
Ogbu, J. U., **13**:48
On Your Own
    assessment, **3**:89
    communication
        disorders, **10**:55
    effective instruction, **4**:73
    emotional disturbance, **11**:55–56
    families/community
        agencies, **5**:63
    fundamentals of special
        education, **1**:51
    gifted and talented child,
        **13**:61–62
    learning disabilities, **9**:65–66
    legal foundations of special
        education, **2**:63
    medical/physical/multiple
        disabilities, **8**:73–74
    mental retardation, **12**:79
    public policy/school
        reform, **6**:53
    sensory disabilities, **7**:69–71
Ooms, T., **5**:42 (tab)
Operant conditioning,
    **4**:38, **4**:65
Opportunity-to-learn (OTL)
    standards, **4**:46, **6**:12,
    **6**:33, **6**:45
Oppositional behavior
    (noncompliance),
    **11**:22–24, **11**:47
Optacons, **4**:52–53
Optical character recognition (OCR),
    **7**:36 (tab), **7**:38, **7**:61
Oral communication,
    for students with
        vision/hearing impairments,
        **7**:39–40, **7**:39 (tab)
Organizations (resources)
    assessment, **3**:93
    communication disorders,
        **10**:58–59
    effective instruction, **4**:77
    emotional disturbance,
        **11**:63–65

fundamentals of special
    education, **1**:54–55
gifted and talented child, **13**:65
learning disabilities, **9**:68–69
medical/physical/multiple
    disabilities, **8**:83–84
mental retardation, **12**:86–87
public policy/school reform,
    **6**:56–57
sensory disabilities, **7**:79–85
transitions, **5**:68
Orientation, **7**:14, **7**:61
Ornstein, A. C., **4**:5–6
Orr, A. L., **7**:7, **7**:11, **7**:13,
    **7**:14, **7**:15, **7**:34
Orr, S., **4**:5
Orthopedic impairments,
    **8**:17–18, **8**:65
    prevalence of, **8**:18
Orthopedic or other health
    impairments, **1**:16–17, **1**:42
Orthosis, **8**:52, **8**:65
Osborn, J., **9**:28
OSEP (Office of Special Education
    Programs), **6**:13–14, **6**:45
Osteogenesis imperfecta, **8**:20, **8**:65
Osteomyelitis, **8**:21, **8**:65
O'Sullivan, P. J., **5**:18
OTL (Opportunity-to-learn)
    standards, **4**:46, **6**:12, **6**:33, **6**:45
Outcomes-based
    accountability, **3**:23, **6**:35

Pace, **4**:13, **4**:65
*Panitch v. State of Wisconsin,*
    **2**:40 (tab)
Parental participation, **6**:29
Partially sighted, **7**:61
*PASE v. Hannon,* **2**:41 (tab)
Passive observation, **3**:29
Pathsounder, **4**:55
Paul, P. V., **7**:23, **7**:24,
    **7**:27, **7**:40, **7**:42
Paulson, F., **3**:39
Paulson, P., **3**:39
Peavey, K. O., **7**:11, **7**:15
Peck, C. A., **12**:55
Peer tutoring, **4**:46–47, **4**:65

Peer tutoring, classwide,
    **4:**47, **4:**63
Peer-directed learning, **4:**46
*Pennsylvania Association of Retarded
    Citizens v. Commonwealth of
    Pennsylvania,* **12:**65–66
PEP (protection in evaluation
    procedures), **1:**13, **1:**42,
    **2:**21–23, **2:**56
Perceptual-motor development,
    **3:**47–48
Perceptual-motor interviews, **3:**48
Perceptual-motor observations, **3:**48
Perceptual-motor tests, **3:**47–48, **3:**80
Performance assessment,
    **3:**24, **3:**80
Perret, Y. M., **8:**22, **8:**47
Perseveration errors, **3:**38, **3:**48
Perspective
    assessment, **3:**73–74
    communication disorders,
        **10:**35–38
    effective instruction, **4:**59–60
    emotional disturbance, **11:**39–41
    fundamentals, **1:**37–38
    gifted and talented, **13:**47–49
    learning disabilities, **9:**53–54
    legal foundations, **2:**51–52
    medical/physical/multiple
        disabilities, **8:**55–59
    mental retardation, **12:**65–68
    public policy/school reform,
        **6:**37–42
    sensory disabilities, **7:**47–51
    transitions, **5:**51–52
Petit mal seizures, **8:**23, **8:**65
Pfiffner, L. J., **9:**44
Phenylketonuria (PKU),
    **12:**14, **12:**72
Phonetic cues, **9:**29, **9:**57
Phonology, **10:**10–11, **10:**44
Physical disabilities, **8:**17–31
    autism, **8:**28–31
    craniofacial anomalies, **8:**22
    defining, **8:**65
    juvenile rheumatoid
        arthritis, **8:**20
    Legg-Calvé-Perthes disease, **8:**21

limb deficiencies, **8:**21–22
multiple sclerosis, **8:**20–21
muscular dystrophy, **8:**19–20
neurological disorders, **8:**22–25
orthopedic impairments, **8:**17–18
osteogenesis imperfecta, **8:**20
poliomyelitis, **8:**18–19
traumatic brain injury, **1:**17, **1:**43,
    **8:**25–28, **8:**66
Physical disruptions, **11:**27, **11:**47
Pilmer, S. L., **8:**15
Pogrund, R. L., **7:**7, **7:**11
Poliomyelitis, **8:**18–19, **8:**65
Portfolios, **3:**26, **3:**39, **3:**80
Post-school interventions, **5:**50, **5:**56
Post-school transitions,
    **5:**23, **5:**24–25, **5:**37
Poteet, J., **3:**21
Powers, M. D., **8:**29, **8:**30
Pragmatics, **10:**11, **10:**44
Pratt, S., **8:**30
Precision teaching, **4:**39, **4:**65
Prereferral interventions
    defining, **1:**9, **1:**22, **1:**42, **3:**80
    determining eligibility, **1:**22
    evolution of, **1:**11–12
    growth in population receiving,
        **1:**19–20
    individualized education
        programs
        (*See* Individualized
        education programs)
    perspective on, **1:**37–38
    process evaluation, **1:**24
    purpose of, **3:**11
Preschool
    attendance increase, **5:**9–10
    early intervention during, **5:**9–10
    Individuals With Disabilities
        Education Act and, **5:**10–12,
        **5:**11 (fig)
    transition to K-12 education
        system, **5:**18–19
    Ypsilanti Perry Preschool Project,
        **5:**15–16
President's Commission on
    Excellence in Special
    Education, **1:**13

Private school, 2:42 (tab),
  2:46–47, 2:54
Process disorders, 9:19, 9:57
Program evaluation
  defining, 3:80
  large-scale, 3:16–17
  teacher's own, 3:17
Programmed learning,
  13:37, 13:39, 13:53
Progress evaluation, 1:24, 3:80
Prostheses/prosthetic devices,
  4:56–57, 4:65, 8:65
Protection in evaluation procedures
  (PEP), 1:13, 1:42, 2:21–23, 2:56
Psychoeducational
  assessment, 3:9, 3:81
Psychological development,
  assessing, 3:45–47
  personality tests, 3:45
  psychological interviews, 3:46–47
  psychological observations,
    3:45–46
Psychological interviews, 3:46–47
Public Law 94–142. See
  Education for All
  Handicapped Children Act
Public policy
  impact on special education,
    6:39–40
  political effects on, 6:10–11
  See also School reform
Pupil unit allocation method,
  6:16–17
Purcell, J. H., 13:45

Quay, H., 3:46

Rakes, T., 3:21
Randomization without
  replacement, 4:60
RAP mnemonic, 4:45
Rapport, establishing, 60
Reading, improving
  analytical programs for,
    9:27, 9:56
  fostering motivation/interest,
    9:30–32
  reading comprehension, 9:28–30

sight word recognition, 9:28
  taped texts for, 9:6
  whole language programs for,
    9:27, 9:57
Reading Excellence Act, 6:20
Reading First, 2:30–31, 6:10, 6:20
Reality therapy, 4:43, 4:65
Reber, M., 8:30
Receptive language, 10:44
Redl, F., 4:44
Referral, 1:22, 1:42
  See also Prereferral interventions
Reflection
  assessment, 3:3–4, 3:85–87
  communication disorders,
    10:5, 10:51
  effective instruction, 4:4, 4:70
  emotional disturbance, 11:3–4,
    11:51–52
  families/community agencies,
    5:3–4, 5:59–60
  fundamentals of special
    education, 1:4, 1:48
  gifted and talented
    child, 13:3–4, 13:57–58
  learning disabilities,
    9:3–4, 9:62
  legal foundations of special
    education, 2:4, 2:60
  medical/physical/multiple
    disabilities, 8:3, 8:69–70
  mental retardation, 12:3–4,
    12:75–76
  public policy/school
    reform, 6:3, 6:49
  sensory disabilities, 7:3, 7:65
Regular education initiative (REI),
  6:21, 6:45
Rehabilitation Act, 2:53, 9:44
Reichert, E. S., 13:45
Reis, S. M., 13:45
Related services, 1:26, 5:12, 10:42
  as part of individualized
    education program,
    1:23, 11:45, 12:33
  defining, 1:42–43, 6:45
  growth in numbers receiving,
    1:19–20

mandated, **1:**31, **2:**48, **6:**40,
      **8:**17, **8:**43, **12:**9
Related services personnel,
      **1:**20, **3:**12
Reliability, **3:**50, **3:**81
Reliability coefficient,
      **3:**50, **3:**81
Remedial education, **3:**10, **3:**81
Renzulli, J., **13:**18, **13:**43
Representativeness, **3:**50–51, **3:**81
Residual functioning,
      **8:**52–53, **8:**65
Resources
      assessment, **3:**91–93
      communication disorders,
            **10:**57–59
      effective instruction, **4:**75–77
      emotional disturbance, **11:**57–65
      families/community agencies,
            **5:**65–68
      fundamentals of special
            education, **1:**53–55
      gifted and talented child,
            **13:**63–65
      learning disabilities, **9:**67
      legal foundations of special
            education, **2:**65–66
      medical/physical/multiple
            disabilities, **8:**75–83
      mental retardation, **12:**81–87
      public policy/school reform,
            **6:**55–57
      sensory disabilities, **7:**73–85
Respondent conditioning,
      **4:**38, **4:**65
Response to intervention (RTI),
      **9:**17, **9:**18
Rheumatic fever,
      **8:**11 (tab), **8:**65
Rogers, C., **4:**44
Rogers, M., **4:**49
Rogers, P. A., **7:**7, **7:**11,
      **7:**13, **7:**14, **7:**15, **7:**34
Rose, L. C., **11:**39
Rotation errors, **3:**48
RTI (response to intervention),
      **9:**17, **9:**18
Rubrics, **3:**31

Rusch, F., **5:**24
Ryser, G., **7:**15

Saccuzzo, D. P., **13:**45
Safe schools, **6:**28–29
Samuelowicz, K., **4:**5
Schaller, J., **7:**15
Schattman, R., **12:**59
Schnur, E., **5:**15
School reform, **6:**19–35
      Goals 2000 (*See* Goals 2000: The
            Educate America Act)
      impact on special
            education, **6:**35
      inclusion as, **6:**21, **6:**38–39
      national goals, **6:**19–20
      national standards, **6:**30–33
      opportunity-to-learn standards,
            **4:**46, **6:**12, **6:**33, **6:**45
      regular education
            initiative/inclusion, **6:**21
      school restructuring,
            **6:**33–34, **6:**45
      *See also* Public policy
School restructuring,
      **6:**33–34, **6:**45
School-based enterprises, **5:**46, **5:**56
Schoolhouse giftedness, **13:**43, **13:**53
Schrier, E. M., **7:**36
Schumaker, J., **4:**45
Schweinhart, L., **5:**16
Screening, **3:**7–8
      defining, **3:**81
      early, **3:**8–9
      late, **3:**9–10
      tests for, **3:**28
      *See also* Protection in evaluation
            procedures
Section 504 of the Rehabilitation
      Act, **2:**11 (tab), **2:**13,
      **2:**14–15, **2:**56, **4:**54
Seizures
      grand mal (tonic-clonic),
            **8:**23, **8:**64
      petit mal, **8:**23, **8:**65
Self-Assessment/Answer Key
      assessment, **3:**1–3,
            **3:**83–85, **3:**87

communication disorders, **10**:1–5,
  **10**:47–51, **10**:53–54
effective instruction, **4**:1–3,
  **4**:67–69, **4**:71
emotional disturbance, **11**:1–3,
  **11**:49–51, **11**:53
families/community agencies,
  **5**:1–3, **5**:57–59, **5**:61
fundamentals of
  special education,
  **1**:1–4, **1**:45–47, **1**:49
gifted and talented child, **13**:1–3,
  **13**:55–57, **13**:59
learning disabilities, **9**:1–3,
  **9**:59–61, **9**:63
legal foundations of
  special education,
  **2**:1, **2**:57–60, **2**:61
medical/physical/multiple
  disabilities, **8**:1–3,
  **8**:67–69, **8**:71
mental retardation, **12**:1–3,
  **12**:73–75, **12**:77
public policy/school reform,
  **6**:1, **6**:47–49, **6**:51
sensory disabilities, **7**:1–3,
  **7**:63–65, **7**:67
Self-care, **12**:47, **12**:57
Self-contained class, **4**:28, **4**:65
Self-determination, **12**:64, **12**:72
Self-direction, **12**:46–47
Self-help skills, **3**:42
Semantics, **10**:11, **10**:44
Sensitivity errors, **3**:62
Sensorineural hearing loss, **7**:19, **7**:61
Sensory acuity, assessing,
  **3**:39–**3**:41 (fig)
Sensory disabilities, teaching
  student with
  assistive listening, **7**:41
  collaboration role in, **7**:52
  communication system, **7**:41–42
  cued speech, **7**:40–41
  eliminating barriers overview,
    **7**:34–38, **7**:35 (tab)–36 (tab),
    **7**:39 (tab)
  empowering student, **7**:47–48
  fostering independence, **7**:42–45

future of, **7**:52
improving communication
  overview, **7**:39 (tab)
oral communication, **7**:39–40
positive interaction tips, **7**:44–45
sign systems, **7**:40
supporting accommodations for,
  **7**:49–51
technology to eliminate barriers,
  **7**:34, **7**:36–38
telecommunication devices, **7**:41
total communication, **7**:40
understanding characteristics
  specific to, **7**:49
*See also* Deaf-and-blind/
  deaf-blind; Hearing
  impairments; Visual
  impairments
Sentner, S. M., **4**:5
Severe disabilities, teaching student
  with, **12**:53–59
  communication considerations,
    **12**:56–57
  community living and, **12**:57–58
  curriculum considerations, **12**:56
  defining severe disabilities,
    **12**:54–55
  instructional approaches,
    **12**:58–59
  mobility, **12**:57
  prevalence of, **12**:55
  self-care and, **12**:57
Shape distortions, **3**:48
Sheltered/supported employment,
  **5**:25, **5**:56
Shin, H., **6**:33
Siblings, effect of exceptionalities
  on, **5**:36–37
Sickle-cell anemia, **8**:11 (tab), **8**:66
Sigafoos, J., **7**:26
Sign language, **7**:39 (tab), **7**:40
Silverman, L. K., **13**:44
Singleton, P., **7**:47
Site-based management,
  **6**:34, **6**:35, **6**:46
Six-hour retarded child, 41
Skilled examiner, **3**:59–61
Skinner, D., **4**:5

Skull fractures, **8:**26, **8:**66
Smith, J., 14–15
*Smith v. Robinson,* **2:**42 (tab), **2:**47–49
Snellen Wall Chart, **3:**40
Social interactions, improving
 for student with emotional
  disturbance, **11:**13–14
 for student with learning
  disabilities, **9:**39–41
 Social problems, **11:**17, **11:**47
 Social skills, **7:**15
 occupational skills and, **3:**42
 school adaptive behavior and,
  **12:**45–46
 training in, **4:**47–48, **4:**65, **12:**45–46
Social values, affect on special
  education, **6:**8–10
Software
 math, **12:**41
 sight word recognition, **9:**28
Sonicguide, **4:**56
Spastic cerebral palsy, **8:**23–24
Special education
 categories of, **1:**15–17
 current reforms in, **6:**40
  (*See also* Public policy;
  School reform)
 defining, **1:**43
 future of, **6:**41
 social values and, **6:**8–10
 *See also* Special education,
  economic factors driving
Special education, economic factors
  driving, **6:**13–17
 allocation methods, **6:**16–17
 federal review of state
  plans, **6:**14
 funding competition, **6:**15
 OSEP programs, **6:**13–14
 research priorities, **6:**15
Special education process. *See*
 Prereferral interventions
Special educators, continuing
 demand for, **1:**20
Specific learning disabilities
 defining, **1:**17, **1:**43
 *See also* Learning disabilities
Spectrum disorder, **8:**29

Speece, D., **9:**17–18
Speech disorders, **10:**44
 articulation disorder, **10:**9–10
 fluency disorder, **10:**10
 voice disorder, **10:**10
Speech evaluation, **10:**44
Speech or language impairments,
 **1:**17, **1:**43
Speech-language pathologist,
 **10:**17–18, **10:**39–41, **10:**44
Spina bifida, **8:**24, **8:**66
Spinal cord injuries, **8:**24–25, **8:**66
Spooner, F., **12:**43
Stahl, S. A., **9:**28
Standard behavior chart, **4:**39, **4:**65
Standards
 defining, **6:**31, **6:**46
 legislation on, **6:**37–38
 national, **6:**30–33
 opportunity-to-learn, **4:**46, **6:**12,
  **6:**33, **6:**45
Stark, J., **10:**27
Stem, B., **12:**43
Stereotypes, **3:**56, **3:**81
Stern, B., **12:**43
Stern, J., **6:**13
Sternberg, R. J., **13:**43
Strabismus, **7:**10, **7:**61
Strichart, S. S., **5:**26
Structured interview, **3:**30
Stuart, M., **7:**29
Student progress records,
 **4:**26 (fig)–27
Stuttering. *See* Fluency disorder
Subdural hematomas, **8:**26, **8:**66
Summative evaluation, **4:**23, **4:**65
Supported employment, **5:**25, **5:**56
Swan, M., **13:**33
Syntax, **10:**10–11
Synthetic speech devices, **7:**37, **7:**62

TA (transactional analysis),
 **4:**44, **4:**65
Talented, defining, **13:**53
TASH (The Association for Persons
 with Severe Handicaps), **12:**55
Task analysis, **3:**22, **3:**81, **4:**10, **4:**40,
 **4:**65, **12:**43–45, **12:**72

Task avoidance, **11**:31–33, **11**:47
Task Force on DSM-IV, **9**:45 (tab)
Taylor, R. L., **3**:7
Teacher
  egalitarian, **4**:59–60
  highly qualified, **2**:31–32
  humanitarian, **4**:60
  radomizer, **4**:60
Teacher education/professional
    development, **6**:26–27
Teacher training, reform in, **6**:40
Teacher unit allocation method, **6**:16
Teaching
  defining, **4**:5, **4**:7, **4**:66
  precision, **4**:39
  principles for effective, **4**:5–6
  tips for, **6**:42
Technical career programs, **5**:45–46
Technology, to increase
    communication/motility,
    **4**:53–54
Technology dependent, **8**:15–16, **8**:66
Tech-prep programs, **5**:45–46, **5**:56
Telecommunication devices, **4**:51–52,
    **4**:66, **7**:39 (tab), **7**:41, **7**:42
Temper tantrums, **11**:47
Terman, L., **13**:20, **13**:41, **13**:42
Test, D. W., **12**:43
Test modifications, **4**:54
Testing/tests
  achievement, **3**:37, **3**:77
  criterion-referenced, **3**:28–29,
      **3**:77–78, **4**:9, **4**:64
  defining, **3**:25, **3**:81
  diagnostic, **3**:28, **3**:78
  formal, **3**:27, **3**:79
  group-administered, **3**:27, **3**:79
  group/individual tests, **3**:27
  informal measures, **3**:27
  norm-/criterion-referenced tests,
      **3**:28–29
  norm-referenced, **3**:29,
      **3**:80, **4**:9, **4**:64
  screening/diagnostics, **3**:28
  test content, **3**:29
  test development, **3**:52–54
  test fairness, **3**:55–56
  test formats, **3**:27–28
  test modifications, **4**:54

The Association for Persons
    with Severe Handicaps
    (TASH), **12**:55
Thematic units, **9**:57
Thinking skills, **4**:19–20
Thomas, D., **5**:15
Thurlow, M. L., **3**:71, **5**:18,
    **6**:9, **6**:33
Thurlow, M. L., Wiley, H. I.,
    & Bielinski, J., **6**:60
Time sampling recording,
    **3**:46, **3**:81
*Timothy W. v. Rochester,
    New Hampshire, School District,*
    **2**:5–6, **2**:42 (tab)–43 (tab)
*Tinker v. Des Moines Independent
    Community School District,*
    **2**:36 (tab)–37 (tab)
Tonic-clonic (grand mal) seizures,
    **8**:23, **8**:64
Total communication, for student
    with vision/hearing
    impairments, **7**:39 (tab), **7**:40
Transactional analysis (TA),
    **4**:44, **4**:65
Transition plans, **5**:17–18
  individualized, **2**:26, **2**:55–56,
      **5**:23, **5**:56, **12**:63, **12**:71
Transition services, **2**:26, **2**:33,
    **2**:56, **5**:6
  defining, **5**:23, **5**:56
  *See also* Community collaboration
Transitions
  effect on families, **5**:36–37
  *See also* Transition plans;
      Transition services;
      Transitions, types of
Transitions, types of, **5**:17–23
  continued education, **5**:26–27
  dropping out, **5**:20–23, **5**:21 (tab)
  during school, **5**:19
  employment/financial
      independence, **5**:24–25
  everyday, **5**:19
  post-school, **5**:23, **5**:24–25, **5**:37
  preschool to K-12 education
      system, **5**:18–19
  within general education
      classrooms, **5**:20

Traumatic brain injury (TBI), **1**:17, **1**:43, **8**:17, **8**:25–28, **8**:66
Tuberculosis, **8**:11 (tab), **8**:66
20/20 vision, **7**:8

Udvari-Solner, A., **12**:67
Unified system, **6**:35, **6**:46
Unstructured interview, **3**:30
U.S. Congress, **2**:16
U.S. Department of Education, **1**:11, **1**:15, **1**:19–20, **7**:10, **7**:11, **7**:21, **7**:30, **7**:56–58, **8**:6, **8**:29, **8**:34, **9**:14 (tab), **12**:11, **12**:61
U.S. Office of Civil Rights, **6**:46
Uslan, M. M., **7**:36

Validity, **3**:51–54, **3**:81
VanDeventer, P., **12**:67
Visual acuity, **3**:40, **7**:8, **7**:62
Visual functioning, **7**:10
Visual impairments, **1**:16, **1**:40
  academic/cognitive characteristics of, **7**:11–14, **7**:54–55
  appropriate literacy medium, **7**:16
  behavioral characteristics of, **7**:14–15
  brief history of special education and, **7**:7
  communication characteristics of, **7**:15–16
  defining, **7**:6, **7**:8, **7**:9, **7**:62
  eligibility for students with, **7**:9–10, **7**:55
  environmental modifications for, **7**:13
  focusing difficulties, **7**:9–10
  physical characteristics of, **7**:14
  prevalence of, **7**:10–11, **7**:54
  signs of, **7**:12 (tab)
  teaching modifications for, **7**:13–14
  teaching tips, **7**:16 (tab)
  technological aid for, **7**:13
  visual functioning, **7**:10
Vocabulary, defining, **10**:45
Voice disorder, **10**:10, **10**:45

Wagner, M., **5**:22, **5**:24
Walker, H. M., **3**:46
Walker, R., **6**:34
Wang, M. C., **4**:31–32
Ward, M., **4**:53
Wards of court/homeless child, **2**:34
Warner, M., **4**:45
*Washington v. Davis*, **2**:39 (tab)
*Watson v. City of Cambridge, Mass.*, **2**:36 (tab)
Web sites (resources)
  effective instruction, **4**:75
  sensory disabilities, **7**:73
Weber, J., **11**:36
Wehman, P., **5**:44–45
Weikart, D., **5**:16
Weiss, J. A., **5**:18
Wheelchairs, **4**:56
Whole language program, **9**:27, **9**:57
Whorton, D., **4**:46
Wiederholt, L., **3**:37
Withdrawal, **3**:47, **11**:6, **11**:13
Wittrock, M. C., **4**:12
Work portfolios, **3**:31
Work-sample assessment, **3**:26, **3**:81
Written expression, improving
  checklists, **9**:33–34
  defining, **10**:45
  familiar words, **9**:34–35
  focus on quantity, **9**:33
  self-evaluation, **9**:34
  software, **9**:35
  timed exercises, **9**:35
*Wyatt v. Stickney*, **2**:38 (tab)

Yell, M. L., **2**:19 (fig), **2**:29, **2**:49–50
Yost, D. S., **4**:5
Young, C .L., **9**:17
Youth apprenticeships programs, **5**:45, **5**:56
Ypsilanti Perry Preschool Project, **5**:15–16
Ysseldyke, J. E., **3**:14, **3**:23, **3**:71, **4**:5, **5**:18, **6**:9, **6**:33, **12**:62

*Zobrest v. Catalina Foothills School District*, **2**:43 (tab)

**CORWIN
PRESS**

The Corwin Press logo—a raven striding across an open book—represents the union of courage and learning. Corwin Press is committed to improving education for all learners by publishing books and other professional development resources for those serving the field of PreK–12 education. By providing practical, hands-on materials, Corwin Press continues to carry out the promise of its motto: **"Helping Educators Do Their Work Better."**